Happiness

Discover the Transformative Power of True Happiness: Unlocking the Secrets to a Fulfilling Life with Proven Strategies and Practical Tips for Lasting Self-Improvement - A Comprehensive Guide to Achieving Inner Peace, Overcoming Adversity, and Living Your Best Life Yet!

Lance P. Richards

Happiness: Discover the Transformative Power of True Happiness: Unlocking the Secrets to a Fulfilling Life with Proven Strategies and Practical Tips for Lasting Self-Improvement - A Comprehensive Guide to Achieving Inner Peace, Overcoming Adversity, and Living Your Best Life Yet!

Table of Contents

01: Introduction: What is True Happiness?

Happiness is something we all crave, yet it can be so elusive. We often find ourselves chasing after it, only to be left feeling empty and unfulfilled. But what is true happiness? And how can we achieve it?

At its core, true happiness is a state of being that comes from within. It is not something that can be bought or acquired through external means. It is a deep sense of contentment and satisfaction that arises from living a life that is aligned with our values and purpose.

In today's world, we are constantly bombarded with messages that suggest that happiness is something we can buy or achieve through external means. We are told that we need to have the latest gadgets, the newest car, or the trendiest clothes in order to be happy. We are bombarded with images of perfect bodies, flawless skin, and seemingly perfect lives on social media. All of this creates a sense of inadequacy and a constant desire to acquire more, do more, and be more.

But the truth is that these external things can only provide us with temporary happiness. They may give us a sense of pleasure or satisfaction in the moment, but they do not provide lasting fulfillment. True happiness comes from within, and it is something that we can cultivate through our thoughts, actions, and attitudes.

In this book, we will explore the transformative power of true happiness and unlock the secrets to living a fulfilling life. We will provide you with proven strategies and practical tips for lasting self-improvement, and guide you on a journey of inner peace, overcoming adversity, and living your best life yet.

Our aim is to help you discover the true meaning of happiness and how to cultivate it in your life. We believe that happiness is not a destination, but rather a journey. It is a process of self-discovery and personal growth that requires effort and commitment. But the rewards are immeasurable.

Throughout this book, we will provide you with the tools and resources you need to embark on this journey. We will explore the science of happiness, the benefits of positive thinking, and the power of gratitude. We will also discuss the role of mindfulness, meditation, and other self-care practices in promoting happiness and well-being.

In addition, we will provide you with practical tips for building strong relationships, setting goals, and living a life that is aligned with your values and purpose. We believe that by following these strategies, you can unlock the transformative power of true happiness and live a fulfilling life that is full of joy, purpose, and meaning.

So, if you are ready to embark on this journey of self-discovery and personal growth, then let's begin. Together, we can unlock the secrets to true happiness and live our best lives yet!

02: The Science of Happiness: Understanding the Basics

Happiness is a universal goal. We all seek it in different ways, and we all have different definitions of what it means to be happy. Yet despite its elusiveness, happiness is something that we can cultivate and nurture within ourselves. With the right mindset, strategies, and practices, we can achieve a lasting sense of joy and contentment that transcends temporary pleasures and external circumstances.

In recent years, the study of happiness has gained momentum in the field of positive psychology. Positive psychology is a branch of psychology that focuses on human strengths, virtues, and optimal functioning, rather than on pathology and illness. It aims to enhance well-being and promote positive emotions, relationships, and achievements.

In this chapter, we will delve into the science of happiness, exploring the basics of positive psychology and its key findings. We will also discuss the main theories of happiness, the factors that influence it, and the practical strategies for increasing happiness in our lives.

02: THE SCIENCE OF HAPPINESS: UNDERSTANDING THE BASICS

Positive Psychology: An Overview

Positive psychology emerged as a field of study in the late 1990s, with the publication of the book "Flow" by Mihaly Csikszentmihalyi and the American Psychological Association's Task Force on Positive Psychology report in 2000. Since then, positive psychology has gained widespread attention and has become a significant force in the study of well-being and human flourishing.

Positive psychology focuses on three main areas: positive emotions, positive traits, and positive institutions. Positive emotions include joy, gratitude, hope, and awe, among others. Positive traits are personal qualities that contribute to well-being and success, such as optimism, resilience, and kindness. Positive institutions are organizations and communities that promote the well-being of their members, such as schools, workplaces, and governments.

The aim of positive psychology is to promote well-being and prevent psychological disorders by fostering positive emotions, traits, and institutions. Positive psychology interventions aim to increase happiness, reduce stress and anxiety, and enhance relationships and personal growth.

02: THE SCIENCE OF HAPPINESS: UNDERSTANDING THE BASICS

Theories of Happiness

There are several theories of happiness, each of which offers a different perspective on what it means to be happy and how we can achieve it. Some of the main theories are:

Hedonic theory: This theory defines happiness as the experience of pleasure and the absence of pain. According to this theory, the goal of life is to maximize pleasure and minimize pain. Hedonic happiness is often associated with material possessions, social status, and sensory pleasures, such as food, sex, and drugs.

Eudaimonic theory: This theory defines happiness as the experience of living a meaningful and purposeful life. Eudaimonic happiness is often associated with personal growth, self-discovery, and fulfilling relationships. According to this theory, the goal of life is to pursue one's unique talents and strengths, and to contribute to the well-being of others.

Self-determination theory: This theory emphasizes the importance of autonomy, competence, and relatedness in achieving happiness. According to this theory, people are happiest when they have control over their lives, feel competent in their skills and abilities, and have positive relationships with others.

Broaden-and-build theory: This theory suggests that positive emotions broaden our thoughts and actions, allowing us to build resources and skills that contribute to long-term well-being. According to this theory, positive emotions, such as joy, gratitude, and love, help us to become more creative, flexible, and resilient.

Factors that Influence Happiness

Happiness is influenced by a variety of factors, including genetics, personality, life circumstances, and intentional activities. Some of the key factors are:

Genetics: Research has shown that genetics play a significant role in determining our baseline level of happiness. However, genetics are not the only factor, and we can still increase our happiness through intentional activities.

Personality: Certain personality traits, such as optimism, extraversion, and conscientiousness, are associated with higher levels of happiness. However, personality is not fixed and can be developed through intentional activities and practice.

Life circumstances: Life circumstances, such as income, health, and social support, can affect our happiness. However, research has shown that these factors account for only a small portion of our overall happiness, and that we can still increase our happiness even in adverse circumstances.

Intentional activities: Intentional activities are actions that we can take to increase our happiness, such as practicing gratitude, engaging in meaningful activities, and building positive relationships. These activities have been shown to increase happiness and well-being over time.

Practical Strategies for Increasing Happiness

Based on the science of happiness, there are several practical strategies that we can use to increase our happiness and well-being. Some of these strategies include:

Practicing gratitude: Gratitude is a powerful emotion that can increase our happiness and well-being. We can cultivate gratitude by keeping a gratitude journal, expressing gratitude to others, and focusing on the positive aspects of our lives.

Engaging in meaningful activities: Meaningful activities are those that give us a sense of purpose and fulfillment. We can engage in meaningful activities by pursuing our passions and interests, volunteering, and contributing to our communities.

Building positive relationships: Positive relationships are a key factor in happiness and well-being. We can build positive relationships by investing in our existing relationships, making new connections, and being kind and compassionate to others.

Practicing mindfulness: Mindfulness is the practice of being present and aware of our thoughts, feelings, and sensations without judgment. Mindfulness can reduce stress and anxiety, increase happiness and well-being, and improve our relationships.

Engaging in physical activity: Physical activity is not only good for our physical health but also for our mental health.

Exercise has been shown to increase happiness and reduce stress and anxiety.

Conclusion

Happiness is a complex and multifaceted concept, but it is something that we can cultivate and nurture within ourselves. Positive psychology has provided us with valuable insights into the science of happiness and practical strategies for increasing well-being. By practicing gratitude, engaging in meaningful activities, building positive relationships, practicing mindfulness, and engaging in physical activity, we can increase our happiness and live a more fulfilling life.

03: The Benefits of Happiness: How It Can Transform Your Life

Happiness is a universal goal that is often the driving force behind our actions and decisions. It is a state of being that is characterized by positive emotions, contentment, and a sense of fulfillment. Happiness is not just a fleeting feeling but rather a way of life that can transform every aspect of our existence.

In this chapter, we will explore the benefits of happiness and how it can transform your life. We will examine the impact of happiness on your physical health, mental well-being, relationships, and overall success. By the end of this chapter, you will have a deeper understanding of why happiness is so important and how you can cultivate it in your own life.

Physical Health

One of the most significant benefits of happiness is its impact on our physical health. Numerous studies have shown that happiness can improve our overall well-being, boost our immune system, and even increase our life expectancy.

03: THE BENEFITS OF HAPPINESS: HOW IT CAN TRANSFORM YOUR LIFE

When we are happy, our bodies release endorphins, which are natural painkillers that help to reduce stress and anxiety. These endorphins also help to strengthen our immune system, making us less susceptible to illness and disease. In fact, a study conducted by the University of Illinois found that happy people are less likely to get sick and more likely to recover quickly when they do.

Happiness can also reduce the risk of heart disease and stroke. A study published in the European Heart Journal found that people who are happy and satisfied with their lives are 22% less likely to develop heart disease than those who are unhappy. Additionally, a study conducted by the American Heart Association found that happy people have lower levels of inflammation, which is a key factor in the development of cardiovascular disease.

Mental Well-Being

In addition to its physical benefits, happiness can also have a profound impact on our mental well-being. Happiness is closely linked to positive emotions, which can help to reduce stress and anxiety and improve our overall mood.

03: THE BENEFITS OF HAPPINESS: HOW IT CAN TRANSFORM YOUR LIFE

When we are happy, we are more likely to have a positive outlook on life, which can help us to cope with difficult situations and overcome adversity. Happiness can also help to improve our self-esteem and self-confidence, which can have a positive impact on our relationships and our overall sense of well-being.

Research has also shown that happiness can improve our cognitive function, including our memory and concentration. A study published in the Journal of Happiness Studies found that happy people are better at problem-solving and have a more flexible thinking style, which can help them to adapt to new situations more easily.

Relationships

Happiness can also have a significant impact on our relationships. When we are happy, we are more likely to have positive interactions with others, which can help to strengthen our social connections and improve our overall sense of well-being.

Happy people are more likely to have fulfilling and supportive relationships, which can provide them with a sense of belonging and purpose. Additionally, happy couples are more likely to have successful and long-lasting relationships, as they are better able to communicate effectively and resolve conflicts in a positive manner.

Success

Finally, happiness can also have a significant impact on our overall success in life. When we are happy, we are more likely to be productive, motivated, and focused, which can help us to achieve our goals and reach our full potential.

Research has shown that happy people are more successful in their careers, earning higher salaries and achieving greater levels of success than their unhappy counterparts. Additionally, happy people are more likely to be resilient in the face of challenges and setbacks, which can help them to persevere and achieve their goals in the long-term.

Conclusion

In conclusion, happiness is a transformative state of being that can have profound benefits for our physical health, mental well-being, relationships, and overall success in life.

03: THE BENEFITS OF HAPPINESS: HOW IT CAN TRANSFORM YOUR LIFE

By cultivating happiness in our own lives, we can improve our overall sense of well-being, boost our immunity, and live longer, healthier lives. We can also improve our mental function, enhance our relationships, and achieve greater success in our personal and professional lives.

The benefits of happiness are clear, but how can we cultivate it in our own lives? Here are some proven strategies and practical tips for lasting self-improvement:

Practice gratitude. Take time each day to reflect on the things in your life that you are grateful for. This can help you to focus on the positive and appreciate the good things in your life.

Engage in activities that bring you joy. Whether it's a hobby, exercise, or spending time with loved ones, make time for activities that bring you happiness and fulfillment.

Build strong relationships. Nurture your relationships with family and friends and invest time in building new connections. Positive social interactions can boost your mood and overall sense of well-being.

03: THE BENEFITS OF HAPPINESS: HOW IT CAN TRANSFORM YOUR LIFE

Practice mindfulness. Engage in activities such as meditation or deep breathing exercises to help you stay present in the moment and reduce stress and anxiety.

Practice self-care. Take care of yourself both physically and mentally by eating a healthy diet, getting enough sleep, and engaging in activities that promote relaxation and self-care.

Set and work towards achievable goals. Having a sense of purpose and working towards achievable goals can help to boost your motivation and overall sense of happiness and fulfillment.

In conclusion, happiness is a transformative state of being that can have a profound impact on every aspect of our lives. By cultivating happiness through gratitude, engaging in activities that bring us joy, building strong relationships, practicing mindfulness, engaging in self-care, and setting achievable goals, we can live our best lives yet.

04: The Pursuit of Happiness: Myths and Misconceptions

Happiness is something that we all want. It's a state of mind that we seek, a feeling of joy and contentment that we hope to experience. But despite its universal appeal, happiness is also something that is often misunderstood. There are many myths and misconceptions that surround the pursuit of happiness, and these can make it difficult for people to achieve lasting happiness in their lives. In this chapter, we'll explore some of the most common myths and misconceptions about happiness and discover the truth about what it takes to be truly happy.

Myth #1: Happiness is a Destination

One of the most pervasive myths about happiness is that it's something that we can achieve if we just work hard enough. We tend to think of happiness as a destination, a place that we can arrive at if we do all the right things. We believe that once we get that promotion, find the perfect partner, or achieve some other goal, we'll finally be happy. But the truth is that happiness is not a destination; it's a journey.

Happiness is not something that we can achieve once and

then forget about. It's something that we need to work on every day, through the ups and downs of life. Happiness is not something that we can achieve through external circumstances alone. It's something that we need to cultivate within ourselves, through our thoughts, feelings, and behaviors.

Myth #2: Happiness is a Constant State

Another common myth about happiness is that it's a constant state. We tend to think that once we're happy, we'll stay that way forever. But the reality is that happiness, like any other emotion, is fleeting. It comes and goes, and we need to learn to ride the waves of our emotions, rather than trying to hold on to happiness forever.

It's important to remember that happiness is not the absence of negative emotions. We all experience sadness, anger, and other difficult emotions from time to time. But we can still be happy overall, even when we're experiencing these emotions. Happiness is not about being happy all the time; it's about finding joy and contentment in the midst of life's challenges.

04: THE PURSUIT OF HAPPINESS: MYTHS AND MIS-CONCEPTIONS

Myth #3: Money Can Buy Happiness

Many people believe that money can buy happiness. We think that if we just had more money, we'd be happier. But the truth is that money can only buy temporary happiness. Material possessions can bring us pleasure and enjoyment in the short-term, but they don't provide lasting happiness.

Research has shown that once our basic needs are met, additional income doesn't necessarily lead to more happiness. In fact, people who prioritize money and material possessions are often less happy than those who focus on relationships, experiences, and personal growth.

Myth #4: Happiness is the Absence of Problems

Another common misconception about happiness is that it's the absence of problems. We tend to think that if we could just eliminate all of our problems and challenges, we'd finally be happy. But the reality is that problems and challenges are a natural part of life, and we can't avoid them altogether.

Happiness is not about having a problem-free life; it's about learning to deal with problems in a positive way. It's about developing resilience and a positive mindset that allows us to navigate life's challenges with grace and ease.

Myth #5: Happiness is Selfish

Finally, there's a common belief that pursuing happiness is selfish. We tend to think that if we focus on our own happiness, we're neglecting the needs of others. But the truth is that happiness is not a zero-sum game. When we prioritize our own happiness, we're actually better able to help others and make a positive impact in the world.

Research has shown that happier people are more likely to engage in pro-social behaviors, such as volunteering, donating to charity, and helping others in need. When we're happy, we have more energy, optimism, and compassion to share with others.

In fact, prioritizing our own happiness can actually be a selfless act. When we take care of ourselves and cultivate our own inner peace and well-being, we become better equipped to support and uplift those around us.

04: THE PURSUIT OF HAPPINESS: MYTHS AND MIS-CONCEPTIONS

The pursuit of happiness is not a selfish endeavor; it's a fundamental human right. We all deserve to be happy, and we all have the capacity to cultivate happiness in our lives. By debunking these common myths and misconceptions, we can start to see happiness as the transformative and empowering force that it truly is.

So, what does it take to be truly happy? The answer is not a simple one, as happiness means different things to different people. However, there are some proven strategies and practical tips that can help us cultivate happiness in our lives.

First and foremost, it's important to cultivate a positive mindset. This means learning to focus on the good in our lives, rather than dwelling on the negative. We can do this by practicing gratitude, which involves intentionally focusing on the things we're thankful for each day. We can also learn to reframe our negative thoughts and emotions in a more positive light, looking for opportunities for growth and learning in every challenge.

Another key to happiness is cultivating healthy relationships. Human beings are social creatures, and we thrive on

04: THE PURSUIT OF HAPPINESS: MYTHS AND MIS-CONCEPTIONS

connection and community. This means investing time and energy in our relationships with family, friends, and loved ones, and also seeking out new connections and opportunities for social engagement.

Finally, happiness also involves pursuing our passions and finding purpose in our lives. This means identifying our values and goals, and working towards them with passion and commitment. Whether it's pursuing a fulfilling career, engaging in creative hobbies, or contributing to a cause we believe in, finding meaning and purpose in our lives is essential for long-term happiness and fulfillment.

In conclusion, the pursuit of happiness is a complex and multifaceted journey that requires intentional effort and ongoing commitment. By debunking the myths and misconceptions that surround happiness, and by practicing proven strategies and practical tips, we can all unlock the transformative power of true happiness and live our best lives yet.

05: Defining Success: How It Relates to Happiness

Success and happiness are two concepts that are often linked together, but they are not the same thing. While success can bring happiness, it is not a guarantee. Happiness is an inner state of contentment and well-being, while success is typically defined by external achievements, such as wealth, power, or status. In this chapter, we will explore how success and happiness are related, and how to define success in a way that aligns with our values and promotes lasting happiness.

The Relationship Between Success and Happiness

There is no denying that success can bring happiness. Achieving a long-term goal, receiving recognition for hard work, or experiencing financial security can all be sources of happiness. However, the relationship between success and happiness is not straightforward. Studies have shown that people who focus solely on external measures of success, such as money or fame, are less likely to be happy than those who focus on internal measures of success, such as personal growth or relationships.

One reason for this is that external measures of success are often beyond our control. We may work hard for years to achieve a promotion, only to be passed over for someone else. Or we may accumulate wealth, but find that it does not bring the happiness we expected. On the other hand, internal measures of success, such as personal growth or meaningful relationships, are within our control. They do not rely on external factors, and they can bring lasting happiness.

Defining Success

Given the complex relationship between success and happiness, it is important to define success in a way that aligns with our values and promotes lasting happiness. To do this, we need to shift our focus from external measures of success to internal ones.

One approach is to define success in terms of our personal goals and values. What do we want to achieve in life, and why? What values are important to us, and how can we live in accordance with them? By setting goals that align with our values, we can create a sense of purpose and meaning in our lives, which can lead to lasting happiness.

05: DEFINING SUCCESS: HOW IT RELATES TO HAPPINESS

Another approach is to define success in terms of personal growth. Instead of focusing on external achievements, we can focus on developing our skills, knowledge, and character. This can include learning new things, facing our fears, or developing our emotional intelligence. By focusing on personal growth, we can create a sense of progress and fulfillment in our lives, which can lead to lasting happiness.

Finally, we can define success in terms of our relationships with others. This can include our family, friends, colleagues, or community. By investing in our relationships and building meaningful connections with others, we can create a sense of belonging and support, which can lead to lasting happiness.

Conclusion

Success and happiness are two concepts that are often linked together, but they are not the same thing. While success can bring happiness, it is not a guarantee. To promote lasting happiness, it is important to define success in a way that aligns with our values and promotes personal growth and meaningful connections with others. By doing so, we can create a sense of purpose, progress, and fulfillment in

05: DEFINING SUCCESS: HOW IT RELATES TO HAPPI-NESS

our lives, which can lead to true happiness.

06: The Power of Positive Thinking: The Role of Mindset in Happiness

Happiness is not just an emotion, but a state of being that is essential to living a fulfilling life. While some people may believe that happiness is something that is outside of their control, the truth is that our mindset plays a huge role in our ability to experience happiness. This chapter explores the power of positive thinking and how it can transform our lives for the better.

The Importance of Mindset

Our mindset is the lens through which we view the world. It shapes our thoughts, feelings, and actions, and can have a profound impact on our overall wellbeing. A positive mindset can help us to overcome adversity, achieve our goals, and experience greater happiness and fulfillment in our lives.

Unfortunately, many people have a negative mindset that is based on fear, self-doubt, and limiting beliefs. This can hold them back from reaching their full potential and experiencing the joys of life. The good news is that with practice, anyone can develop a positive mindset that is rooted in optimism, gratitude, and a belief in their own abilities.

The Power of Positive Thinking

Positive thinking is the practice of focusing on the good in life, rather than dwelling on the negative. This doesn't mean that we ignore our problems or challenges, but rather that we approach them with a constructive attitude and a belief that we can overcome them. By cultivating a positive mindset, we can transform our lives in a number of ways.

Improved Health and Wellbeing

Research has shown that positive thinking can have a powerful impact on our physical and mental health. A positive mindset can boost our immune system, reduce stress, and improve our overall sense of wellbeing. People who practice positive thinking are also more likely to engage in healthy behaviors such as exercise, healthy eating, and getting enough sleep.

Greater Resilience

Life is full of ups and downs, and it's inevitable that we will face challenges and setbacks along the way. However, a positive mindset can help us to bounce back from adversity more quickly and effectively. By focusing on solutions rather than problems, we can approach challenges with a sense of resilience and determination.

Increased Success

A positive mindset can also help us to achieve our goals and reach our full potential. When we believe in ourselves and our abilities, we are more likely to take risks and pursue our dreams. This can lead to greater success in all areas of life, from career and finances to personal relationships and hobbies.

Practical Strategies for Developing a Positive Mindset

If you're ready to start cultivating a more positive mindset, there are a number of strategies that you can try:

Practice gratitude: Take time each day to reflect on the things that you're grateful for. This can be as simple as a roof over your head, a good meal, or a supportive friend. By focusing on the positive aspects of your life, you can shift your mindset towards gratitude and appreciation.

Challenge negative thoughts: When you catch yourself having negative thoughts, challenge them with evidence to the contrary. For example, if you're feeling like a failure, remind yourself of times when you've succeeded in the past. By reframing negative thoughts in a more positive light, you can change the way you view yourself and the world around you.

Surround yourself with positivity: Seek out positive people, books, and media that inspire and uplift you. This can help you to stay motivated and focused on your goals, even during challenging times.

Practice self-care: Take care of your physical and emotional needs by getting enough sleep, eating well, and engaging in activities that bring you joy. When you feel good, you're more likely to have a positive outlook on life.

Visualize success: Take time each day to visualize yourself achieving your goals and living your best life. By focusing on a positive future, you can create the motivation and momentum needed to turn your dreams into reality.

06: THE POWER OF POSITIVE THINKING: THE ROLE OF MINDSET IN HAPPINESS

Learn from mistakes: Instead of dwelling on your failures and mistakes, use them as opportunities for growth and learning. By reframing your failures as learning experiences, you can approach challenges with a more positive and constructive mindset.

Practice mindfulness: Mindfulness is the practice of being present in the moment and fully engaged in what you're doing. By practicing mindfulness, you can reduce stress, improve your focus, and cultivate a more positive outlook on life.

By incorporating these strategies into your daily routine, you can start to transform your mindset and experience greater happiness and fulfillment in your life.

The Role of Positive Thinking in Overcoming Adversity

Positive thinking is especially important during times of adversity and challenge. When we face difficult circumstances, it's easy to become overwhelmed with negative thoughts and emotions. However, by cultivating a positive mindset, we can approach challenges with a greater sense of resilience and determination.

For example, if you're dealing with a health issue, it's important to focus on the positive aspects of your life, such as the support of your loved ones and the progress you've already made towards recovery. By reframing your mindset in a more positive light, you can approach your health challenge with a greater sense of hope and optimism.

Similarly, if you're facing financial difficulties, it's important to focus on the steps you can take to improve your situation, rather than dwelling on the negative aspects of your finances. By taking a proactive approach and focusing on solutions, you can overcome financial obstacles and achieve greater financial stability in the future.

The Power of Positive Thinking in Building Relationships

Positive thinking can also have a powerful impact on our relationships with others. When we approach our relationships with a positive and constructive mindset, we are more likely to communicate effectively, resolve conflicts, and build strong, healthy relationships.

For example, if you're experiencing conflict with a loved one, it's important to approach the situation with an open mind and a willingness to listen and understand their perspective. By focusing on solutions rather than blame, you can work together to find a resolution that works for both of you.

Similarly, if you're building new relationships, it's important to approach them with a positive and open mindset. By focusing on the positive aspects of the other person, you can build a strong foundation of trust and mutual respect that will lead to a fulfilling and meaningful relationship.

Conclusion

The power of positive thinking cannot be overstated. By cultivating a positive mindset, we can transform our lives in countless ways, from improving our health and wellbeing to achieving our goals and building strong relationships with others. While it may take time and practice to develop a positive mindset, the benefits are well worth the effort. So start practicing gratitude, challenge your negative thoughts, surround yourself with positivity, and visualize your success. With a positive mindset, you can unlock the transformative power of true happiness and live your best life yet.

07: Gratitude and Appreciation: The Importance of Counting Your Blessings

Gratitude and appreciation are two powerful tools that can transform our lives and help us achieve true happiness. When we focus on the positive aspects of our lives and learn to appreciate what we have, we can overcome adversity, find inner peace, and live our best life yet.

In this chapter, we will explore the importance of gratitude and appreciation and how they can help us overcome obstacles, increase our well-being, and strengthen our relationships with others. We will also provide practical tips and strategies for cultivating gratitude and appreciation in our daily lives, so we can experience the transformative power of true happiness.

The Power of Gratitude and Appreciation

Gratitude and appreciation are often used interchangeably, but they are slightly different concepts. Gratitude is the act of feeling and expressing thankfulness for the blessings we have received in our lives, while appreciation is the act of recognizing and valuing the positive qualities of people, things, or experiences.

Research has shown that practicing gratitude and appreciation can have a significant impact on our well-being. Studies have found that people who regularly practice gratitude
experience more positive emotions, have a greater sense of
purpose, and are more resilient in the face of adversity.
They also tend to have stronger relationships and a higher
level of overall life satisfaction.

In contrast, people who focus on what they don't have or
take their blessings for granted tend to experience more
negative emotions, have a lower sense of well-being, and are
less resilient when faced with challenges. They may also
struggle with feelings of envy, jealousy, and dissatisfaction,
which can lead to a cycle of negative thinking and behaviors.

The Benefits of Cultivating Gratitude and Appreciation

Cultivating gratitude and appreciation can have a wide
range of benefits, including:

Increased well-being: Research has shown that people who

regularly practice gratitude and appreciation have a higher level of overall well-being, including more positive emotions, a greater sense of purpose, and improved physical health.

Reduced stress: Gratitude and appreciation can help us cope with stress and anxiety by shifting our focus from negative thoughts to positive ones. When we focus on what we are grateful for, we are less likely to feel overwhelmed or stressed by the challenges we face.

Improved relationships: Gratitude and appreciation can strengthen our relationships with others by helping us recognize and value the positive qualities of the people in our lives. When we express our gratitude and appreciation to others, we build stronger connections and deepen our bonds.

Increased resilience: Gratitude and appreciation can help us become more resilient in the face of adversity. When we focus on what we are grateful for, we are better able to cope with challenges and bounce back from setbacks.

Enhanced empathy: Gratitude and appreciation can increase our empathy and compassion for others by helping us recognize and value the positive qualities of those around us. When we appreciate the good in others, we are more likely to treat them with kindness and understanding.

Practical Tips for Cultivating Gratitude and Appreciation

If you want to experience the transformative power of true happiness, it's essential to cultivate gratitude and appreciation in your daily life. Here are some practical tips to get you started:

Keep a gratitude journal: Take a few minutes each day to write down three things you are grateful for. This simple practice can help you focus on the positive aspects of your life and increase your sense of well-being.

Practice mindfulness: Mindfulness is the practice of being present in the moment without judgment. By practicing mindfulness, you can learn to appreciate the small moments in life and find joy in the present.

Express gratitude to others: Take the time to thank the people in your life who have made a positive impact on you.

07: GRATITUDE AND APPRECIATION: THE IMPORT-ANCE OF COUNTING YOUR BLESSINGS

Whether it's a handwritten note, a phone call, or a kind gesture, expressing gratitude to others can strengthen your relationships and increase your own sense of well-being.

Focus on the good: When you find yourself focusing on negative thoughts or experiences, try to shift your focus to the positive aspects of your life. Instead of dwelling on what went wrong, focus on what went right or what you learned from the experience.

Practice random acts of kindness: Doing something kind for someone else can be a powerful way to cultivate gratitude and appreciation. Whether it's buying a cup of coffee for a stranger or volunteering your time, acts of kindness can help you feel more connected to others and increase your sense of well-being.

Create a gratitude jar: Find a jar or container and decorate it in a way that makes you happy. Each day, write down something you are grateful for on a small piece of paper and place it in the jar. Over time, you will have a collection of positive memories and experiences to look back on when you need a boost of positivity.

07: GRATITUDE AND APPRECIATION: THE IMPORTANCE OF COUNTING YOUR BLESSINGS

Reflect on past experiences: Take some time to reflect on past experiences that you are grateful for. This could be a positive memory from childhood, a special moment with a loved one, or an accomplishment that you are proud of. Reflecting on these experiences can help you feel more positive and grateful in the present moment.

Practice self-compassion: It's important to practice gratitude and appreciation for yourself as well as others. Take some time each day to acknowledge and appreciate your own positive qualities and accomplishments.

Incorporating these practices into your daily life can help you cultivate a greater sense of gratitude and appreciation, leading to a more fulfilling and happy life.

Conclusion

Gratitude and appreciation are powerful tools that can transform our lives and help us achieve true happiness. By focusing on the positive aspects of our lives and learning to appreciate what we have, we can overcome adversity, find inner peace, and live our best life yet.

07: GRATITUDE AND APPRECIATION: THE IMPORT-ANCE OF COUNTING YOUR BLESSINGS

In this chapter, we explored the importance of gratitude and appreciation and provided practical tips and strategies for cultivating these qualities in our daily lives. By incorporating these practices into our lives, we can experience the transformative power of true happiness and live a more fulfilling and meaningful life. So, take some time each day to count your blessings and appreciate the good in your life, and watch as your happiness and well-being grow.

08: Cultivating Resilience: Overcoming Adversity and Building Inner Strength

Life is a journey filled with twists and turns, and along the way, we all encounter obstacles and adversity. Sometimes, these challenges can be overwhelming and can lead to feelings of hopelessness and despair. However, it's important to remember that adversity can also be an opportunity for growth and self-discovery.

In this chapter, we'll explore the concept of resilience and how it can help us overcome adversity and build inner strength. Resilience is the ability to bounce back from difficult situations, to adapt to change, and to recover from setbacks. It's a key component of happiness and a critical skill for achieving success in all areas of life.

So, how can we cultivate resilience in ourselves? The following strategies and tips can help:

Develop a Growth Mindset

One of the most important factors in building resilience is having a growth mindset. A growth mindset is the belief that our abilities and intelligence can be developed through hard work, practice, and perseverance. This mindset allows us to view challenges as opportunities for growth and learning, rather than as insurmountable obstacles.

To develop a growth mindset, start by reframing your thoughts and beliefs. Instead of thinking "I can't do this" or "this is too hard," try to think "I can learn how to do this" or "this is a challenge, but I can overcome it." Focus on your progress and your efforts, rather than on your failures or shortcomings.

Practice Self-Care

Taking care of ourselves is essential for building resilience. This means getting enough sleep, eating well, exercising regularly, and taking time to relax and recharge. When we're physically and mentally healthy, we're better equipped to handle stress and adversity.

Self-care also means taking care of our emotional needs. This might involve seeking out support from friends or family, talking to a therapist, or practicing mindfulness and meditation. It's important to prioritize our own well-being and to make self-care a regular part of our routine.

Build a Support Network

Having a strong support network is crucial for building resilience. This network might include friends, family members,
colleagues, or mentors who can offer encouragement, advice, and emotional support during difficult times.

To build a support network, start by reaching out to people
in your life who you trust and respect. Make an effort to
maintain these relationships by staying in touch, expressing
gratitude, and offering support in return. It's also helpful to
join groups or organizations that share your interests or values, as these can provide opportunities to connect with like-
minded individuals.

Practice Gratitude

Gratitude is a powerful tool for building resilience. When
we focus on the positive aspects of our lives, we're better
able to cope with adversity and bounce back from setbacks.

To practice gratitude, take time each day to reflect on the
things you're grateful for. This might include small things

like a sunny day or a good cup of coffee, or larger things like supportive relationships or meaningful work. You can express gratitude through journaling, meditation, or simply sharing your appreciation with others.

Embrace Change

Change is a constant in life, and learning to embrace it can help us build resilience. When we resist change, we create more stress and tension for ourselves. When we embrace it, we open ourselves up to new opportunities and experiences.

To embrace change, try to approach it with a positive attitude. Focus on the potential benefits and opportunities that it might bring, rather than on the challenges or difficulties. Practice flexibility and adaptability, and be open to trying new things and taking risks.

Find Meaning and Purpose

Finding meaning and purpose in our lives can also help us build resilience. When we have a sense of purpose, we're better able to weather the storms of life and stay focused on our goals.

08: CULTIVATING RESILIENCE: OVERCOMING ADVERSITY AND BUILDING INNER STRENGTH

To find meaning and purpose, start by reflecting on your values and what's important to you. Consider what brings you joy and fulfillment, and what you want to contribute to the world. This might involve exploring new hobbies or interests, volunteering in your community, or pursuing a new career path.

When we have a sense of meaning and purpose, we're more motivated to overcome challenges and setbacks. We're also better able to bounce back from difficult situations, knowing that we're working towards something that matters to us.

Practice Resilience-Building Activities

Finally, there are several activities and practices that can help us build resilience. These might include:

– Journaling: Writing down your thoughts and feelings can help you process difficult emotions and gain perspective on challenging situations.

– Mindfulness and meditation: These practices can help you stay centered and focused during times of stress and anxiety.

— Exercise: Regular exercise has been shown to reduce stress and improve mood, which can in turn improve resilience.

— Setting goals: Setting realistic goals can give you a sense of purpose and direction, and can help you stay motivated during difficult times.

— Positive self-talk: Practicing positive self-talk can help you stay optimistic and focused on your strengths and abilities, rather than on your weaknesses and failures.

By incorporating these activities into your daily routine, you can develop the habits and skills necessary to build resilience and overcome adversity.

In conclusion, cultivating resilience is essential for living a fulfilling and happy life. By developing a growth mindset, practicing self-care, building a support network, practicing gratitude, embracing change, finding meaning and purpose, and engaging in resilience-building activities, you can develop the inner strength and resilience necessary to over-

come any obstacle that comes your way. Remember, resilience is not a fixed trait - it's something that can be developed and strengthened with practice and effort. So, take
these strategies and tips to heart, and start building your resilience today!

09: Managing Stress: Coping Strategies for a Happy Life

Stress is an inevitable part of life. Whether you're juggling a career, family, personal goals, or all of the above, there's bound to be moments where the pressure feels overwhelming. However, it's important to remember that stress is not always a bad thing. In fact, a healthy dose of stress can motivate us to be productive, achieve our goals, and grow as individuals.

The problem arises when stress becomes chronic, and we find ourselves unable to cope with the demands of our daily lives. Chronic stress can lead to a range of physical and mental health problems, from heart disease and obesity to depression and anxiety. In this chapter, we'll explore the causes and effects of stress, and offer practical strategies for managing stress and finding inner peace.

Causes of Stress

Stress can be caused by a variety of factors, including:

– Work: Heavy workloads, tight deadlines, and difficult colleagues can all contribute to workplace stress.

09: MANAGING STRESS: COPING STRATEGIES FOR A HAPPY LIFE

– Personal relationships: Relationship issues, family conflict, and social pressure can all cause stress.

– Financial concerns: Money problems, debt, and job loss can all be significant sources of stress.

– Health issues: Chronic illnesses, injuries, and physical limitations can all cause stress.

– Major life changes: Moving, divorce, death of a loved one, and other major life changes can all trigger stress.

Effects of Stress

Stress affects both our physical and mental health. Here are just a few of the ways stress can impact our lives:

– Physical health: Chronic stress can lead to a range of physical health problems, including high blood pressure, heart disease, obesity, and diabetes.

– Mental health: Chronic stress can also take a toll on our mental health, contributing to anxiety, depression, and other mood disorders.

– Sleep: Stress can disrupt our sleep patterns, leading to insomnia or other sleep problems.

– Relationships: Stress can strain our relationships with family, friends, and colleagues, leading to conflict and tension.

– Work performance: Chronic stress can impact our work performance, leading to decreased productivity, burnout, and even job loss.

Strategies for Managing Stress

Fortunately, there are many strategies for managing stress and finding inner peace. Here are some proven techniques for coping with stress:

– Exercise: Exercise is a great way to relieve stress, boost mood, and improve physical health. Aim for at least 30 minutes of exercise a day, such as walking, swimming, or cycling.

– Meditation: Meditation is a powerful tool for calming the mind and reducing stress. Try practicing mindfulness meditation for just a few minutes each day to start.

09: MANAGING STRESS: COPING STRATEGIES FOR A HAPPY LIFE

– Sleep: Getting enough sleep is essential for managing stress. Aim for 7-8 hours of sleep per night, and establish a relaxing bedtime routine.

– Time management: Poor time management can contribute to stress. Use a planner or calendar to schedule your time effectively, and prioritize the most important tasks.

– Social support: Talking to friends, family, or a therapist can help relieve stress and provide emotional support.

– Relaxation techniques: Relaxation techniques such as deep breathing, yoga, or massage can help reduce stress and promote relaxation.

– Hobbies and interests: Pursuing hobbies and interests that you enjoy can provide a healthy outlet for stress and help you relax.

– Healthy diet: Eating a healthy, balanced diet can help improve physical health and reduce stress. Try to incorporate plenty of fruits, vegetables, and whole grains into your diet.

– Avoid unhealthy coping mechanisms: Unhealthy coping mechanisms such as smoking, drinking, or overeating can

actually increase stress levels. Try to avoid these behaviors
and instead focus on healthy coping strategies.

– Take breaks: Taking regular breaks throughout the day
can help reduce stress and improve productivity.

– Practice self-care: Taking care of yourself is essential for
managing stress. Make time for activities that bring you joy,
such as reading, taking a bath, or listening to music.

– Set realistic goals: Setting realistic goals can help you feel
more in control of your life and reduce stress. Break large
goals into smaller, achievable steps.

– Get organized: Being organized can help reduce stress
and increase productivity. Make to-do lists, declutter your
space, and establish a routine.

– Practice gratitude: Focusing on the things you are grateful
for can help shift your perspective and reduce stress. Try
keeping a gratitude journal or simply taking a few minutes
each day to reflect on what you are thankful for.

– Seek professional help: If stress is impacting your daily
life or you are experiencing symptoms of anxiety or depres-

sion, it may be helpful to seek professional help. A therapist or mental health professional can provide support and guidance.

It's important to remember that managing stress is an ongoing process. What works for one person may not work for another, and it may take time to find the strategies that work best for you. Don't be afraid to try new techniques, and be patient with yourself as you work to manage stress and find inner peace.

In conclusion, stress is an inevitable part of life, but it doesn't have to control us. By using the strategies outlined in this chapter, we can learn to manage stress, improve our physical and mental health, and find lasting happiness and fulfillment. Remember, taking care of yourself is not selfish —it's essential for living your best life yet!

10: Self-Compassion: Treating Yourself with Kindness and Understanding

Self-compassion is a powerful tool that can help you live a happier, more fulfilling life. It involves treating yourself with kindness and understanding, just as you would treat a close friend or family member. When you cultivate self-compassion, you become more resilient, better able to cope with adversity, and less likely to fall into the traps of self-criticism and self-judgment that can erode your self-esteem and undermine your well-being.

In this chapter, we'll explore what self-compassion is, why it's important, and how you can develop this skill for yourself. We'll look at the research on self-compassion and its benefits, as well as practical strategies for incorporating self-compassion into your daily life.

What is Self-Compassion?

Self-compassion is a way of relating to yourself that involves three key components: kindness, common humanity, and mindfulness. Kindness means treating yourself with warmth, caring, and concern, rather than harsh criticism or judgment. Common humanity means recognizing that everyone experiences suffering and difficulty at some point in their lives, and that you are not alone in your struggles. Mindfulness means being aware of your thoughts, feelings, and sensations in a non-judgmental way, and staying present with whatever arises in the moment.

When you practice self-compassion, you are not denying or ignoring your pain, but rather acknowledging it with kindness and understanding. This helps to reduce the intensity of negative emotions and increase positive emotions, such as gratitude and joy.

Why is Self-Compassion Important?

Research has shown that self-compassion is strongly associated with mental health and well-being. Studies have found that people who practice self-compassion are less likely to experience depression, anxiety, and stress, and more likely to feel happy, content, and fulfilled in their lives.

Self-compassion is also linked to greater resilience and better coping skills. When you treat yourself with kindness and understanding, you are better able to bounce back from setbacks and challenges, and to persevere in the face of difficulty.

Perhaps most importantly, self-compassion can help you break free from the cycle of self-criticism and self-judgment that can hold you back from achieving your goals and living your best life. When you are kind to yourself, you are more likely to take risks, try new things, and pursue your passions, even in the face of fear or uncertainty.

How to Develop Self-Compassion

Developing self-compassion is a skill that takes time and practice, but it is a skill that anyone can learn. Here are some strategies for cultivating self-compassion in your daily life:

Treat yourself like you would treat a friend

Think about how you would comfort a friend who was going through a difficult time. What would you say to them? How would you show them that you care? Now, try to apply the same kindness and understanding to yourself. Treat yourself as you would treat a friend, with warmth, empathy, and compassion.

Practice mindfulness

Mindfulness can help you become more aware of your thoughts, feelings, and sensations, and stay present with whatever arises in the moment. This can help you respond to difficult situations with greater equanimity and self-compassion. Try practicing mindfulness meditation or simply taking a few deep breaths and tuning in to your body sensations.

Reframe negative self-talk

Notice when you are engaging in negative self-talk or self-criticism. Try to reframe these thoughts in a more compassionate and constructive way. For example, instead of telling yourself "I'm so stupid for making that mistake," try saying "I made a mistake, but everyone makes mistakes sometimes. What can I learn from this experience?"

Practice self-acceptance

Self-compassion requires a fundamental acceptance of yourself, flaws and all. It's important to recognize that everyone has imperfections, and that you don't have to be perfect to be worthy of love and respect. Practice accepting yourself for who you are, rather than constantly striving for an unattainable ideal.

Take care of yourself

Self-compassion involves taking care of yourself, both physically and emotionally. This means getting enough sleep, eating nutritious foods, exercising regularly, and engaging in activities that bring you joy and fulfillment. When you prioritize self-care, you are sending a message to yourself that you are worthy of attention and care.

Connect with others

One of the key components of self-compassion is recognizing our common humanity. Connecting with others can help you feel less alone in your struggles, and provide support and understanding when you need it most. Reach out to friends or family members, or consider joining a support group or community that aligns with your interests.

Practice self-forgiveness

10: SELF-COMPASSION: TREATING YOURSELF WITH KINDNESS AND UNDERSTANDING

Self-forgiveness is an important aspect of self-compassion. It involves recognizing that everyone makes mistakes, and that you are not defined by your past actions or decisions. Practice forgiving yourself for past mistakes or regrets, and focus on moving forward with a sense of self-compassion and growth.

Conclusion

Self-compassion is a transformative tool that can help you live a happier, more fulfilling life. By treating yourself with kindness and understanding, you become more resilient, better able to cope with adversity, and less likely to fall into the traps of self-criticism and self-judgment that can erode your self-esteem and undermine your well-being.

Incorporating self-compassion into your daily life takes practice and commitment, but the benefits are well worth it. By practicing self-compassion, you can cultivate a sense of inner peace, overcome adversity, and live your best life yet. So go ahead, treat yourself with kindness and understanding – you deserve it!

11: Forgiveness: Letting Go of Grudges and Moving Forward

Forgiveness is a powerful tool that can help you let go of grudges, overcome past hurts, and move forward in life with greater peace and happiness. In this chapter, we will explore the transformative power of forgiveness, why it is so important for our mental and emotional well-being, and how you can cultivate forgiveness in your life.

Forgiveness is the act of letting go of anger, resentment, and bitterness towards someone who has wronged you. It does not mean forgetting what happened or excusing the person's behavior. Instead, it is about releasing the negative emotions that are holding you back and making a conscious decision to move on.

The benefits of forgiveness are many. It can improve your mental health by reducing stress, anxiety, and depression. It can also improve your relationships by increasing empathy, compassion, and understanding. Forgiveness can even have physical health benefits, such as lowering blood pressure and reducing the risk of heart disease.

However, forgiveness is not always easy. It can be especially difficult when the wrong that was done to you was severe or when the person who wronged you is not sorry for their actions. It can also be hard to forgive yourself for past mistakes and failures.

The good news is that forgiveness is a skill that can be learned and practiced. Here are some strategies for cultivating forgiveness in your life:

Acknowledge your emotions: The first step towards forgiveness is to acknowledge your emotions. Recognize the pain, anger, and resentment that you are feeling, and allow yourself to experience them without judgment.

Practice empathy: Try to put yourself in the other person's shoes and understand their perspective. This can help you see things from a different angle and increase your compassion towards them.

Let go of expectations: Don't expect the other person to apologize or make amends before you forgive them. Forgiveness is about releasing your own negative emotions, not about changing the other person's behavior.

11: FORGIVENESS: LETTING GO OF GRUDGES AND MOVING FORWARD

Practice self-forgiveness: If you are struggling to forgive yourself for past mistakes or failures, try practicing self-compassion. Treat yourself with the same kindness and understanding that you would offer to a friend.

Seek support: Forgiveness can be a challenging process, and it can be helpful to seek support from a therapist or support group. Talking through your emotions with someone who understands can help you gain new insights and find greater peace.

Practice gratitude: Cultivating gratitude can help you shift your focus from negative emotions to positive ones. Take time each day to reflect on the things that you are grateful for, even in the midst of difficult circumstances.

Be patient: Forgiveness is a process, and it may take time to fully let go of negative emotions. Be patient with yourself and trust that with time and practice, you can cultivate greater forgiveness and inner peace.

In conclusion, forgiveness is a powerful tool for personal growth and well-being. By letting go of grudges and negative emotions, we can free ourselves from the past and move

11: FORGIVENESS: LETTING GO OF GRUDGES AND MOVING FORWARD

forward in life with greater peace, happiness, and fulfillment. With practice and patience, anyone can cultivate forgiveness and live their best life yet.

12: The Art of Mindfulness: Being Present and Finding Joy in the Moment

The world we live in today is fast-paced, hectic, and filled with distractions. It's easy to get caught up in the hustle and bustle of daily life and forget to appreciate the simple things. We're constantly multitasking, trying to juggle work, family, friends, and social media, often neglecting our own well-being in the process. But what if there was a way to slow down, be present, and find happiness in the moment? That's where the art of mindfulness comes in.

Mindfulness is the practice of being fully present in the moment, without judgment or distraction. It's about paying attention to your thoughts, feelings, and surroundings, and experiencing them without trying to change them or react to them. By cultivating mindfulness, you can learn to live in the present moment, reduce stress and anxiety, and find joy in the simple things in life.

In this chapter, we'll explore the art of mindfulness and how it can transform your life. We'll look at the benefits of mindfulness, the science behind it, and practical tips for incorporating mindfulness into your daily routine.

The Benefits of Mindfulness

Mindfulness has been shown to have a wide range of benefits for both your mental and physical health. Here are just a few of the many ways mindfulness can improve your life:

Reducing Stress and Anxiety - Mindfulness helps you stay present in the moment, reducing worry and anxiety about the future or regrets about the past. By focusing on the present moment, you can let go of stress and anxiety, and enjoy a greater sense of calm and peace.

Improving Focus and Concentration - When you practice mindfulness, you learn to focus your attention on the present moment, which can help improve your concentration and focus. This can be especially helpful if you're struggling with distractions at work or school.

Boosting Emotional Well-being - Mindfulness can help you manage difficult emotions, such as anger, fear, and sadness, by allowing you to experience them without getting overwhelmed by them. By developing greater emotional aware-

ness and regulation, you can improve your overall well-being and happiness.

Enhancing Relationships - Mindfulness can also improve
your relationships by helping you communicate more effectively and empathetically with others. By being present and
fully engaged in your interactions, you can build stronger
connections with the people around you.

The Science of Mindfulness

The benefits of mindfulness aren't just anecdotal - they're
backed up by scientific research. Studies have shown that
mindfulness can have a positive impact on a wide range of
health outcomes, including:

Reducing Symptoms of Depression and Anxiety - A meta-
analysis of 39 studies found that mindfulness-based interventions were effective in reducing symptoms of depression
and anxiety.

Improving Cognitive Function - Research has also shown
that mindfulness can improve cognitive function, including
working memory, attention, and executive function.

12: THE ART OF MINDFULNESS: BEING PRESENT AND FINDING JOY IN THE MOMENT

Lowering Blood Pressure - Mindfulness has been shown to lower blood pressure in people with hypertension, which can reduce the risk of heart disease and stroke.

Reducing Chronic Pain - Mindfulness-based interventions have been found to be effective in reducing chronic pain in a variety of conditions, including fibromyalgia, back pain, and headaches.

Practical Tips for Incorporating Mindfulness into Your Daily Routine

If you're interested in incorporating mindfulness into your daily routine, there are many simple and practical tips you can try. Here are a few to get you started:

Start with Small Moments of Mindfulness - You don't have to set aside hours of your day to practice mindfulness. Start with small moments throughout the day, such as taking a few deep breaths before starting a task or paying attention to the sensations in your body while you're walking.

Practice Mindful Breathing - One of the simplest and most effective mindfulness techniques is mindful breathing. Take a few minutes each day to focus on your breath, noticing the sensation of air moving in and out of your body. If your mind wanders, gently bring it back to your breath.

Practice Mindful Eating - When you're eating, try to be fully present and focused on the experience. Notice the colors, textures, and flavors of your food, and savor each bite.

Use Mindfulness Apps - There are many apps available that can guide you through mindfulness exercises, such as Headspace, Calm, and Insight Timer.

Practice Mindful Movement - Yoga, tai chi, and other mindful movement practices can help you cultivate mindfulness while also improving your physical health.

Practice Gratitude - Mindfulness and gratitude go hand in hand. Take a few moments each day to think about things you're grateful for, and focus on the positive aspects of your life.

Practice Self-Compassion - Mindfulness is about being present and accepting of yourself as you are. Practice self-compassion by treating yourself with kindness and understanding, rather than harsh self-criticism.

Incorporating mindfulness into your daily routine takes practice, but the benefits are well worth it. By learning to be present and fully engaged in the moment, you can reduce stress and anxiety, improve your mental and physical health, and find greater joy and fulfillment in your life.

Conclusion

In today's fast-paced world, it's easy to get caught up in the endless distractions and pressures of daily life. But by practicing mindfulness, we can learn to slow down, be present, and find happiness in the moment. Mindfulness has been shown to have a wide range of benefits for both our mental and physical health, and incorporating it into our daily routine is easier than you might think.

Whether you start with small moments of mindfulness throughout the day, practice mindful breathing, or use mindfulness apps, the key is to be present and fully engaged in the moment. By cultivating mindfulness, we can reduce stress and anxiety, improve our relationships and cognitive function, and find greater joy and fulfillment in our lives. So

12: THE ART OF MINDFULNESS: BEING PRESENT AND FINDING JOY IN THE MOMENT

why not give it a try and see how mindfulness can transform your life?

13: Connection and Community: The Importance of Relationships for Happiness

The pursuit of happiness is a fundamental aspect of the human experience. We all want to feel happy and fulfilled, but the path to achieving this can be challenging. One of the most crucial factors in our quest for happiness is our relationships with others. In this chapter, we will explore the importance of connection and community in our lives and how cultivating healthy relationships can lead to a happier and more fulfilling life.

Human beings are social creatures, and our need for connection and belonging is deeply ingrained in our DNA. Studies have shown that social isolation and loneliness can have adverse effects on our physical and mental health, leading to higher rates of depression, anxiety, and even mortality. On the other hand, having strong and supportive relationships can enhance our overall well-being and increase our resilience in the face of adversity.

But what exactly constitutes a healthy relationship? How do we build and maintain meaningful connections with others?

13: CONNECTION AND COMMUNITY: THE IMPORT- ANCE OF RELATIONSHIPS FOR HAPPINESS

The answer lies in understanding the different types of rela- tionships we have and the various factors that contribute to their success.

Family relationships are the first and most significant con- nections we make in life. Our parents, siblings, and exten- ded family members play a vital role in shaping our identity and values, and they often provide us with a sense of be- longing and security. However, family relationships can also be complicated and challenging, and conflicts can arise due to differences in opinions, expectations, and behaviors. Learning how to navigate these challenges and communic- ate effectively with our family members is crucial for main- taining healthy and fulfilling relationships.

Friendships are another essential aspect of our social lives. Unlike family relationships, friendships are based on mu- tual interests, shared experiences, and a sense of ca- maraderie. Friends provide us with emotional support, laughter, and a sense of belonging outside of our immediate family. However, like any relationship, friendships require effort and investment to maintain. It's essential to be a good listener, communicate honestly and openly, and be there for our friends when they need us.

Romantic relationships are perhaps the most complex and intimate connections we can have with another person. Romantic partners share a deep emotional and physical bond, and they rely on each other for companionship, love, and support. However, maintaining a healthy and satisfying romantic relationship requires more than just love and attraction. Communication, trust, mutual respect, and a willingness to compromise are all essential components of a successful partnership.

Finally, community relationships are the connections we have with our larger social networks, such as our neighbors, colleagues, or fellow members of a particular group or organization. These relationships can provide us with a sense of belonging and purpose beyond our immediate family and friends, and they often play a vital role in our personal and professional lives. Volunteering, joining clubs or groups, or attending social events are all great ways to build community relationships and expand our social networks.

Building and maintaining healthy relationships can be challenging, but there are several proven strategies and practical tips that can help. Here are some of the most effective ways to cultivate meaningful connections with others:

Practice active listening: One of the most critical aspects of communication is being an active listener. This means paying attention to what the other person is saying, asking questions, and showing empathy and understanding. Active listening can help us build trust and rapport with others and deepen our relationships.

Communicate openly and honestly: Being able to communicate our thoughts, feelings, and needs clearly and honestly is essential for building healthy relationships. Avoiding conflict or hiding our emotions can lead to resentment and frustration, so it's crucial to express ourselves in a respectful and constructive manner.

Show appreciation and gratitude: Expressing appreciation and gratitude for the people in our lives can go a long way in strengthening our relationships. A simple thank you or compliment can make someone feel valued and appreciated, and it can help us build stronger connections with others.

Be present and attentive: In our fast-paced and technology-

driven world, it's easy to become distracted and disconnec-
ted from the people around us. Being present and attentive
means giving our full attention to the person we're interact-
ing with and engaging in meaningful conversations and
activities.

Practice forgiveness and compassion: No relationship is
perfect, and conflicts and misunderstandings are inevitable.
Practicing forgiveness and compassion can help us overcome these challenges and maintain healthy and fulfilling
relationships. It's essential to let go of grudges, apologize
when necessary, and approach conflicts with an open mind
and heart.

Invest time and effort: Building and maintaining healthy relationships requires time and effort. It's crucial to prioritize
our relationships and make time for the people we care
about. This can mean scheduling regular phone calls or
meetups, planning special activities or trips, or simply
checking in on each other regularly.

Be open to new connections: Building and expanding our
social networks can bring new perspectives, experiences,
and opportunities into our lives. It's essential to be open to

meeting new people and making new connections, whether through work, social events, or other activities.

By cultivating healthy relationships and building strong connections with others, we can enhance our overall well-being and experience greater happiness and fulfillment in life. However, it's essential to remember that building relationships takes time, effort, and patience. It's normal to experience setbacks and challenges along the way, but with the right mindset and strategies, we can overcome these obstacles and create meaningful and lasting connections with the people around us.

In conclusion, connection and community are essential components of a happy and fulfilling life. By understanding the different types of relationships we have and the factors that contribute to their success, we can cultivate healthy and meaningful connections with others. By practicing active listening, communicating openly and honestly, showing appreciation and gratitude, being present and attentive, practicing forgiveness and compassion, investing time and effort, and being open to new connections, we can build and maintain strong and fulfilling relationships that bring joy

13: CONNECTION AND COMMUNITY: THE IMPORT-
ANCE OF RELATIONSHIPS FOR HAPPINESS

and meaning into our lives.

14: Giving Back: The Joy of Helping Others

As humans, we are wired to seek happiness and fulfillment in our lives. We pursue success, wealth, and relationships, hoping that these things will bring us the happiness we crave. But often, even when we achieve these things, we find ourselves still feeling unfulfilled, empty, and lacking in purpose. It is in moments like these that we must turn our attention outward and seek to give back to others.

Giving back is not only a way to help those in need, but it is also a powerful tool for self-improvement and personal growth. When we give back, we tap into a deeper sense of purpose and meaning in our lives, and we discover the transformative power of true happiness.

There are many ways to give back, and no act of kindness is too small. From volunteering at a local soup kitchen to donating money to a charitable organization, there are countless ways to make a positive impact on the world around us. Here are just a few of the many benefits of giving back:

It promotes empathy and compassion: When we give back,

we are forced to step outside of our own lives and consider the needs of others. This helps us develop empathy and compassion for those who may be less fortunate than us.

It builds connections and fosters a sense of community: Giving back often involves working with others, whether that be volunteering with a group or donating to a cause. This helps us build connections with like-minded individuals and fosters a sense of community and belonging.

It boosts self-esteem and confidence: When we give back, we are making a positive difference in the world around us. This can boost our self-esteem and confidence, as we see the impact that our actions are having.

It reduces stress and promotes overall well-being: Studies have shown that giving back can reduce stress and promote overall well-being. When we focus on the needs of others, we take the focus off of our own problems and concerns, which can be a welcome relief.

It provides a sense of purpose and meaning: Giving back can provide a sense of purpose and meaning in our lives. When we feel like we are making a positive difference in the world, we are more likely to feel fulfilled and satisfied with our lives.

So how can we start giving back? Here are some practical tips for incorporating giving back into your life:

Start small: Giving back doesn't have to be a grand gesture. Start small by doing something kind for someone else, such as paying for someone's coffee or holding the door open for someone.

Volunteer: There are countless organizations that rely on volunteers to make a difference in their communities. Find an organization that aligns with your interests and values and see how you can get involved.

Donate: If you don't have the time to volunteer, consider donating to a charitable organization. Even a small donation can make a big difference.

Use your skills: Think about how you can use your skills and talents to make a difference. If you are a writer, consider volunteering to write for a non-profit organization. If you are a musician, consider performing at a charity event.

Get your friends and family involved: Giving back is even

more powerful when you do it with others. Encourage your friends and family to get involved in volunteering or donating to a cause that you care about.

In conclusion, giving back is not only a way to help others, but it is also a powerful tool for personal growth and self-improvement. By tapping into our natural desire to help others, we can discover the transformative power of true happiness and live our best lives yet. So go out there and make a difference, big or small, and see how giving back can change your life for the better.

15: Finding Purpose and Meaning: Aligning Your Life with Your Values

Happiness is not just about feeling good in the moment, but about living a fulfilling life with a sense of purpose and meaning. When you align your life with your values and passions, you can create a life that is not just happy, but also deeply fulfilling. In this chapter, we will explore how to discover your purpose and align your life with your values so that you can experience true happiness and live your best life yet.

The Importance of Finding Purpose and Meaning

When you live a life without purpose or meaning, you may find yourself feeling lost, unfulfilled, or even depressed. You may struggle to find motivation or direction, and may feel like you are just going through the motions of life without really living it. However, when you have a clear sense of purpose and meaning, you can live a life that is deeply fulfilling, and you will find yourself motivated, energized, and excited about your life.

Research has shown that people who have a strong sense of

purpose and meaning in their lives tend to be happier, healthier, and more successful than those who do not. They are more resilient in the face of adversity, and they tend to have better relationships and more fulfilling careers. In fact, having a sense of purpose and meaning has been shown to be a key factor in longevity and overall well-being.

So, how can you discover your purpose and align your life with your values? Here are some proven strategies and practical tips for finding meaning and purpose in your life.

Reflect on Your Values and Passions

The first step in aligning your life with your values is to reflect on what those values are. Ask yourself what is truly important to you in life. What are the things that you value most? Is it family, friends, career, spirituality, health, or something else entirely?

Once you have identified your values, think about what activities or hobbies you enjoy most. What are the things that you are passionate about? What makes you feel energized and alive? Your passions can give you a clue about what your purpose may be.

For example, if you are passionate about helping others, your purpose may be to work in a helping profession such as counseling or social work. If you are passionate about the environment, your purpose may be to work in a field that promotes sustainability or conservation.

Explore Your Options

Once you have identified your values and passions, it's time to explore your options. What careers, hobbies, or activities align with your values and passions? What opportunities are available to you?

Start by doing some research. Look up different careers or hobbies that align with your values and passions. Talk to people who work in those fields or who have similar interests. Attend events or conferences related to your passions or interests.

You may also want to consider volunteering or interning in a field that interests you. This can give you hands-on experience and help you determine if this is truly the path you want to pursue.

15: FINDING PURPOSE AND MEANING: ALIGNING YOUR LIFE WITH YOUR VALUES

Take Action

Once you have identified your purpose and values and explored your options, it's time to take action. This may mean making some changes in your life, such as pursuing a new career or hobby, or it may mean simply making small changes to align your life with your values.

For example, if your value is family, you may want to make more time for your loved ones, or if your value is health, you may want to start exercising or eating healthier. Small changes can add up to big results over time.

It's important to remember that finding your purpose and aligning your life with your values is a journey, not a destination. It may take time and effort to get where you want to be, but the journey itself can be rewarding and fulfilling.

Embrace Your Unique Path

Finally, it's important to remember that your path to purpose and meaning will be unique to you. Don't compare yourself to others or feel like you have to follow a certain formula for success. Your values, passions, and purpose are unique to you, and your journey will be as well.

Embrace your strengths and weaknesses, and don't be afraid to take risks and try new things. You may encounter obstacles or setbacks along the way, but these can be opportunities for growth and learning.

It's also important to be open to change and growth. Your values and passions may evolve over time, and your purpose may shift as well. Don't be afraid to reassess and adjust your goals and plans as needed.

Conclusion

Finding purpose and meaning in your life is a key component of true happiness and fulfillment. By aligning your life with your values and passions, you can create a life that is not just happy, but deeply meaningful and fulfilling.

Reflect on your values and passions, explore your options, and take action to align your life with your purpose. Embrace your unique path, and be open to change and growth. With these strategies and tips, you can discover your purpose and live your best life yet.

16: Pursuing Your Passions: The Role of Hobbies and Creativity in Happiness

Introduction

Life can be stressful, overwhelming, and chaotic. We are constantly bombarded with tasks, responsibilities, and obligations that leave us feeling drained and burnt out. It's easy to get caught up in the daily grind and forget about the things that truly make us happy. Pursuing your passions is one of the most effective ways to find joy and fulfillment in life. In this chapter, we'll explore the role of hobbies and creativity in happiness and provide practical tips for incorporating more passion into your daily routine.

Why Pursuing Your Passions Is Important

Many of us have been conditioned to believe that success and happiness come from working hard and achieving external goals. We believe that if we can just get that promotion, buy that house, or reach that milestone, we'll finally be happy. However, research has shown that happiness is not solely dependent on external factors. In fact, pursuing your passions and engaging in activities that bring you joy can have a profound impact on your overall happiness and well-being.

Here are just a few reasons why pursuing your passions is important:

It provides a sense of purpose and meaning - When you engage in activities that you're passionate about, you feel a sense of purpose and meaning in your life. You're not just going through the motions; you're actively pursuing something that brings you joy and fulfillment.

It promotes creativity and innovation - Pursuing your passions often involves exploring new ideas, trying new things, and pushing the boundaries of what's possible. This mindset can help you approach challenges in your personal and professional life with a more creative and innovative mindset.

It reduces stress and promotes relaxation - Engaging in activities that you're passionate about can help reduce stress and promote relaxation. It's a chance to disconnect from the demands of daily life and focus on something that brings you joy.

16: PURSUING YOUR PASSIONS: THE ROLE OF HOBBIES AND CREATIVITY IN HAPPINESS

It fosters social connections - Pursuing your passions often involves connecting with like-minded individuals who share your interests. This can help you build new friendships and strengthen existing ones.

Now that we've established why pursuing your passions is important, let's explore some practical ways to incorporate more passion into your daily routine.

Finding Your Passions

The first step in pursuing your passions is identifying what they are. This may seem like a daunting task, especially if you're not sure where to start. Here are some tips for discovering your passions:

Make a list of activities that bring you joy - Start by making a list of activities that you enjoy doing. This could include anything from reading to painting to hiking. The key is to focus on activities that bring you joy and make you feel energized.

Try new things - Don't be afraid to try new things. You may discover a passion for something that you never even considered before. Take a cooking class, try rock climbing, or sign up for a dance lesson.

Reflect on your childhood interests - Think back to your childhood and the activities that you enjoyed doing. Were you always drawing or building things? Did you love playing sports or exploring the outdoors? These childhood interests can provide valuable clues about your passions.

Pay attention to what makes you lose track of time - Notice the activities that you get so engrossed in that you lose track of time. These are often the activities that you're most passionate about.

Incorporating Passion into Your Daily Routine

Once you've identified your passions, it's time to incorporate them into your daily routine. Here are some practical tips for doing just that:

Make time for your passions - One of the biggest obstacles to pursuing our passions is lack of time. Make a conscious effort to carve out time in your schedule for the activities that bring you joy. Even if it's just 30 minutes a day, make it a priority.

Set goals - Setting goals can be a powerful motivator when it comes to pursuing your passions. Whether it's completing a painting, running a 5K, or learning a new language, setting specific, measurable goals can help you stay focused and motivated.

Get creative with your schedule - If you're struggling to find time for your passions, think outside the box. Maybe you can wake up 30 minutes earlier to work on a project, or maybe you can squeeze in a workout during your lunch break. Look for ways to make your passions a priority in your daily routine.

Find a community - Connecting with like-minded individuals who share your interests can be a great way to stay motivated and inspired. Join a club, take a class, or attend a workshop related to your passion. You'll not only meet new people, but you'll also have the opportunity to learn new skills and techniques.

Embrace the process - Pursuing your passions is not always easy. There will be times when you feel frustrated, stuck, or

unmotivated. Remember that the journey is just as important as the destination. Embrace the process and enjoy the
ride.

The Benefits of Pursuing Your Passions

Incorporating more passion into your daily routine can have
a profound impact on your overall happiness and well-being. Here are just a few of the benefits:

Increased happiness and fulfillment - Pursuing your passions can bring a sense of joy and fulfillment to your life
that cannot be achieved through external factors alone.

Reduced stress and anxiety - Engaging in activities that
you're passionate about can help reduce stress and anxiety,
providing a much-needed break from the demands of daily
life.

Improved mental and physical health - Pursuing your passions can improve your mental and physical health by promoting relaxation, reducing stress, and increasing physical
activity.

Enhanced creativity and innovation - Pursuing your pas-

16: PURSUING YOUR PASSIONS: THE ROLE OF HOB-BIES AND CREATIVITY IN HAPPINESS

sions can help you approach challenges in your personal and professional life with a more creative and innovative mindset.

Conclusion

Pursuing your passions is a powerful way to find joy and fulfillment in life. By identifying your passions, setting goals, and incorporating passion into your daily routine, you can unlock the transformative power of true happiness. Remember that the journey is just as important as the destination, so enjoy the process and embrace the many benefits of pursuing your passions.

17: Taking Care of Your Body: Physical Health and Its Connection to Happiness

Happiness is a holistic experience that involves different aspects of our lives. To achieve true happiness, we must focus on all areas of our well-being, including our physical health. Our bodies are the vessels that carry us through life, and we must take care of them to live our best lives yet.

Physical health is essential to our overall well-being. When we are physically healthy, we feel more energetic, productive, and confident. It also helps us to maintain a positive outlook on life and face challenges with resilience. Physical health is not just about having a fit and toned body, but it encompasses many aspects of our lives, including exercise, nutrition, sleep, and hygiene.

Exercise is one of the most critical factors in maintaining physical health. Exercise helps to strengthen our muscles, improve our cardiovascular system, and boost our immune system. It also releases endorphins, which are the body's natural feel-good chemicals. Endorphins promote a positive outlook on life and reduce stress levels. Exercise can also help us to maintain a healthy weight, improve our balance, and prevent chronic diseases such as diabetes, heart disease, and obesity.

There are many types of exercises that we can incorporate into our daily routine, including cardio, strength training, and flexibility exercises. Cardio exercises such as running, cycling, or swimming, can help to improve our cardiovascular health, increase our endurance, and reduce the risk of heart disease. Strength training exercises such as weight lifting, push-ups, or squats, can help to build and maintain our muscles, bones, and joints. Flexibility exercises such as yoga or stretching can improve our range of motion, prevent injuries, and reduce stress levels.

Nutrition is another critical factor in maintaining physical health. A well-balanced and nutritious diet can provide our bodies with the necessary nutrients, vitamins, and minerals needed to function correctly. A healthy diet can also help us to maintain a healthy weight, reduce the risk of chronic diseases, and improve our mental health.

A healthy diet should consist of whole foods, including fruits, vegetables, lean proteins, whole grains, and healthy fats. We should limit our intake of processed foods, added sugars, and unhealthy fats. We should also stay hydrated by drinking plenty of water and limit our alcohol consumption.

Sleep is another essential factor in maintaining physical health. Sleep is when our bodies repair and rejuvenate themselves. It also helps to improve our mental health and overall well-being. Lack of sleep can lead to a weakened immune system, decreased cognitive function, and an increased risk of chronic diseases such as diabetes, heart disease, and obesity.

We should aim to get 7-8 hours of sleep every night. We can achieve this by creating a bedtime routine, avoiding screens before bedtime, and creating a comfortable sleep environment.

Hygiene is also a crucial aspect of physical health. Good hygiene habits can help to prevent the spread of germs, bacteria, and viruses, which can cause illness. Good hygiene habits include washing our hands regularly, brushing and flossing our teeth, and bathing regularly.

In conclusion, physical health is an essential component of

overall well-being and happiness. By incorporating regular exercise, a healthy diet, sufficient sleep, and good hygiene habits into our daily routine, we can maintain physical health and achieve lasting happiness. Remember, our bodies are the vessels that carry us through life, and we must take care of them to live our best lives yet.

18: Sleep and Rest: The Importance of Restorative Practices

Introduction

Sleep is an essential part of our lives, and we spend a significant portion of our time doing it. It is crucial to get enough quality sleep to maintain good physical and mental health. The lack of sleep can affect our ability to concentrate, make decisions, and handle stress. In this chapter, we will explore the importance of sleep and rest in our lives, and how to cultivate healthy restorative practices to enhance our overall wellbeing.

The Importance of Sleep

Sleep is an essential function of the body, and it plays a critical role in our physical and mental health. During sleep, our body repairs and regenerates cells, strengthens the immune system, and restores energy levels. Good quality sleep is crucial for maintaining optimal brain function, including memory consolidation and learning.

On the other hand, inadequate sleep can lead to a range of health problems, including obesity, diabetes, cardiovascular disease, and mental health disorders such as depression and anxiety. Chronic sleep deprivation can also lead to decreased productivity, impaired cognitive function, and increased risk of accidents and injuries.

The Benefits of Restorative Practices

Restorative practices are activities that promote relaxation and stress reduction, allowing the body and mind to rest and recharge. These practices can help improve the quality of sleep, reduce stress, and increase feelings of wellbeing.

Some popular restorative practices include:

Yoga: Yoga is a mind-body practice that combines physical postures, breathing exercises, and meditation. It has been shown to reduce stress, improve sleep quality, and increase feelings of calm and relaxation.

Meditation: Meditation is a practice that involves focusing the mind on a specific object, such as the breath or a mantra. It has been shown to reduce stress, anxiety, and depression, and improve sleep quality.

Massage: Massage is a therapeutic practice that involves

manipulating the soft tissues of the body, such as the muscles and connective tissues. It has been shown to reduce stress, improve sleep quality, and relieve muscle tension and pain.

Aromatherapy: Aromatherapy is the use of essential oils to promote relaxation and reduce stress. Essential oils can be diffused, applied topically, or added to a bath. They have been shown to reduce anxiety, improve sleep quality, and enhance feelings of relaxation.

Mindful breathing: Mindful breathing involves focusing the attention on the breath and noticing the sensations in the body. It has been shown to reduce stress, improve sleep quality, and increase feelings of calm and relaxation.

Progressive muscle relaxation: Progressive muscle relaxation involves tensing and relaxing different muscle groups in the body, promoting relaxation and reducing muscle tension. It has been shown to reduce stress, improve sleep quality, and relieve muscle tension and pain.

Tips for Cultivating Restorative Practices

18: SLEEP AND REST: THE IMPORTANCE OF RESTOR-ATIVE PRACTICES

– Make sleep a priority: Set aside enough time for sleep each night, and create a relaxing sleep environment by keeping the room cool, dark, and quiet.

– Develop a bedtime routine: Establish a consistent bedtime routine that includes relaxing activities, such as reading, taking a bath, or listening to calming music.

– Incorporate restorative practices into your daily routine: Make time for restorative practices, such as yoga or meditation, on a regular basis.

– Practice mindful breathing: Take a few moments throughout the day to focus on your breath and notice the sensations in your body.

– Take breaks throughout the day: Schedule breaks throughout the day to rest and recharge. Go for a walk, practice yoga, or simply take a few deep breaths.

– Reduce screen time before bed: Avoid using electronic devices before bedtime, as the blue light emitted by screens can interfere with sleep quality.

Conclusion

18: SLEEP AND REST: THE IMPORTANCE OF RESTORATIVE PRACTICES

In conclusion, sleep and restorative practices are essential for maintaining good physical and mental health. By prioritizing sleep, developing a bedtime routine, and incorporating restorative practices into our daily lives, we can improve our overall wellbeing and live happier, more fulfilling lives.

It is important to remember that restorative practices are not a one-size-fits-all solution. What works for one person may not work for another. It may take some trial and error to find the practices that work best for you. It is also important to be patient and consistent in your practice, as the benefits of restorative practices may not be immediately apparent.

In addition to restorative practices, it is important to practice good sleep hygiene. This includes maintaining a consistent sleep schedule, avoiding caffeine and alcohol before bed, and creating a sleep-conducive environment.

Finally, if you are experiencing chronic sleep problems or other symptoms of sleep disorders, it is important to seek medical advice. A healthcare professional can help diagnose and treat sleep disorders and provide personalized recommendations for improving sleep quality.

18: SLEEP AND REST: THE IMPORTANCE OF RESTORATIVE PRACTICES

In conclusion, sleep and rest are critical components of our overall wellbeing. By prioritizing restorative practices and good sleep hygiene, we can enhance our physical and mental health, reduce stress, and live happier, more fulfilling lives. So, make sure to take the time to rest, recharge, and prioritize your sleep, and experience the transformative power of true happiness.

19: Nutrition and Happiness: The Link Between Food and Mood

Nutrition and Happiness: The Link Between Food and Mood

We've all heard the phrase, "you are what you eat," but did you know that what you eat can also affect your mood? It's true, the food we consume can have a significant impact on our mental health and emotional well-being. In this chapter, we'll explore the relationship between nutrition and happiness, and how you can use food to boost your mood and increase your overall sense of well-being.

The Science Behind the Link Between Food and Mood

To understand the link between food and mood, it's essential to know a bit about the science behind it. Our brains are complex organs that require specific nutrients to function correctly. The neurotransmitters in our brains, such as serotonin, dopamine, and norepinephrine, are responsible for regulating our moods and emotions. These neurotransmitters are made from specific amino acids that are obtained from the food we eat.

19: NUTRITION AND HAPPINESS: THE LINK BETWEEN FOOD AND MOOD

For example, serotonin is made from the amino acid tryptophan, which is found in foods such as turkey, chicken, and bananas. Dopamine is made from the amino acid tyrosine, which is found in foods such as almonds, avocados, and eggs. By consuming foods that contain these essential amino acids, we can help to support the production of these neurotransmitters, which can lead to increased feelings of happiness and well-being.

In addition to supporting the production of neurotransmitters, certain foods can also have a direct impact on our moods. For example, research has shown that consuming foods that are high in sugar and processed carbohydrates can lead to feelings of fatigue, irritability, and even depression. On the other hand, consuming foods that are high in healthy fats, such as omega-3 fatty acids, can help to boost our mood and reduce feelings of anxiety and stress.

The Impact of Nutrition on Mental Health

It's not just our moods that are affected by nutrition; our overall mental health is also impacted by the foods we eat. Research has shown that individuals who consume a diet that is high in processed foods and unhealthy fats are more likely to experience symptoms of depression and anxiety. In contrast, those who consume a diet that is rich in fruits, vegetables, whole grains, and lean proteins are less likely to experience these symptoms.

In addition to improving our mood and mental health, a healthy diet can also help to reduce the risk of developing chronic diseases such as heart disease, diabetes, and cancer. These diseases can have a significant impact on our mental health and well-being, so by consuming a healthy diet, we can help to protect ourselves from these conditions and improve our overall quality of life.

Practical Tips for Incorporating Nutrition into Your Happiness Journey

Now that we've established the link between nutrition and happiness let's explore some practical tips for incorporating nutrition into your happiness journey.

Focus on Whole Foods: Rather than relying on processed and packaged foods, focus on consuming whole foods that are nutrient-dense and unprocessed. This means consuming foods such as fruits, vegetables, whole grains, lean proteins, and healthy fats.

Incorporate Omega-3 Fatty Acids: Omega-3 fatty acids are essential for supporting brain health and mood regulation. Incorporate foods such as salmon, sardines, chia seeds, and walnuts into your diet to ensure that you're getting enough of these important nutrients.

Limit Processed Carbohydrates: Consuming foods that are high in sugar and processed carbohydrates can lead to feelings of fatigue and depression. Instead, focus on consuming complex carbohydrates such as whole grains, fruits, and vegetables.

Stay Hydrated: Dehydration can lead to feelings of fatigue and irritability. Make sure that you're staying hydrated throughout the day by drinking plenty of water and consuming hydrating foods such as watermelon, cucumbers, and celery.

Mindful Eating: Practicing mindful eating can help you to tune into your body's hunger and fullness signals and ensure that you're consuming the right amount of nutrients for your body's needs. Take the time to savor your food, chew slowly, and pay attention to how your body feels as you eat.

Consider Supplementation: While it's best to obtain all of your nutrients from whole foods, sometimes it can be challenging to get enough of certain nutrients through diet alone. Consider taking supplements such as a multivitamin or omega-3 supplement to ensure that you're getting all of the nutrients your body needs.

Experiment with Healthy Recipes: Eating healthy doesn't have to be boring! Experiment with new recipes and ingredients to find healthy meals and snacks that you enjoy. Pinterest and food blogs are great resources for finding healthy recipes that are easy to prepare.

Avoid Restrictive Diets: While it's important to focus on consuming healthy foods, it's also important to avoid overly restrictive diets. Restricting certain foods or food groups can lead to feelings of deprivation and ultimately lead to unhealthy food behaviors. Instead, focus on balance and moderation, and allow yourself to indulge in your favorite foods in moderation.

Seek Professional Help: If you're struggling with disordered eating or have specific dietary needs, consider seeking professional help from a registered dietitian. A registered dietitian can help you to develop a healthy eating plan that meets your specific needs and ensures that you're getting all of the nutrients your body needs.

In Conclusion

Nutrition and happiness are intricately linked, and by focusing on consuming a healthy and balanced diet, we can boost our mood, support our mental health, and improve our overall quality of life. By incorporating the tips outlined in this chapter, you can start to use nutrition to support your happiness journey and live your best life yet!

20: Mind-Body Connection: The Benefits of Exercise for Mental Health

The mind and the body are intricately connected, and research has shown that physical exercise can have a significant impact on mental health. Exercise is not just good for the body; it is also good for the mind. In fact, exercise has been proven to be one of the most effective ways to combat depression, anxiety, and other mental health issues.

Exercise has a variety of benefits for mental health, including reducing stress and anxiety, improving mood, increasing self-esteem, and boosting cognitive function. The benefits of exercise on mental health are well documented, and many people have experienced these benefits firsthand.

One of the main ways that exercise improves mental health is by reducing stress and anxiety. Exercise has been shown to reduce levels of the stress hormone cortisol, which can have a significant impact on mental health. When cortisol levels are high, people are more likely to experience symptoms of anxiety and depression. By reducing cortisol levels, exercise can help to alleviate these symptoms.

Exercise has also been shown to have a positive effect on mood. When we exercise, our brains release endorphins, which are natural feel-good chemicals. These endorphins can help to boost mood and reduce symptoms of depression. In fact, exercise has been shown to be just as effective as antidepressant medications for some people.

Another way that exercise improves mental health is by increasing self-esteem. When we exercise, we feel better about ourselves and our bodies. This can lead to increased self-confidence and self-esteem, which can have a positive impact on mental health. Additionally, exercise can help to improve body image, which is often a source of anxiety for many people.

Exercise can also have a positive impact on cognitive function. Studies have shown that exercise can improve memory, attention, and other cognitive functions. This is because exercise increases blood flow to the brain, which can help to improve brain function. Additionally, exercise can help to protect the brain from age-related decline.

There are many different types of exercise that can have a positive impact on mental health. Aerobic exercise, such as

running, cycling, or swimming, has been shown to be particularly effective. This type of exercise increases heart rate
and breathing, which can help to reduce stress and anxiety.
Additionally, strength training exercises, such as weightlift-
ing, can help to improve mood and increase self-esteem.

It is important to note that exercise should be part of a holistic approach to mental health. While exercise can be effective in reducing symptoms of depression and anxiety, it
is not a cure-all. It is important to also seek professional
help, such as therapy or medication, if needed.

In addition to the mental health benefits of exercise, there
are also many physical health benefits. Exercise can help to
reduce the risk of many chronic diseases, such as heart disease, diabetes, and obesity. It can also help to improve overall fitness and stamina.

Getting started with exercise can be challenging, especially
if you are not used to being active. However, there are many
ways to incorporate exercise into your daily routine. This
can include taking a walk during your lunch break, going for
a run in the morning, or joining a fitness class.

20: MIND-BODY CONNECTION: THE BENEFITS OF EXERCISE FOR MENTAL HEALTH

In conclusion, the mind and the body are connected, and exercise has been shown to have a significant impact on mental health. Exercise can help to reduce stress and anxiety, improve mood, increase self-esteem, boost cognitive function, and improve physical health. While exercise is not a cure-all for mental health issues, it can be an effective tool for reducing symptoms and improving overall well-being.

21: The Power of Laughter: Finding Joy and Humor in Life

Laughter is an essential part of human nature. It is a universal language that transcends cultural barriers, connects people, and creates a sense of community. But laughter is much more than just a social lubricant. It has the power to transform our lives, heal our bodies and minds, and make us happier, healthier, and more resilient.

In this chapter, we will explore the transformative power of laughter and its many benefits for our physical, emotional, and mental well-being. We will also discuss practical tips and strategies for incorporating more laughter and humor into our lives, even during challenging times.

The Science of Laughter

Laughter is a complex physiological response that involves various regions of the brain, including the cerebral cortex, limbic system, and brainstem. When we laugh, our brain releases endorphins, which are natural painkillers and mood enhancers. These feel-good chemicals help to reduce stress, boost our immune system, and promote overall well-being.

21: THE POWER OF LAUGHTER: FINDING JOY AND HUMOR IN LIFE

Studies have shown that laughter has many health benefits, including:

— Reducing stress: Laughter triggers the release of endorphins, which help to reduce the production of stress hormones like cortisol and adrenaline.

— Boosting the immune system: Laughter increases the production of antibodies and activates T-cells, which help to fight off infections and diseases.

— Relieving pain: Laughter releases endorphins, which act as natural painkillers and can help to reduce chronic pain.

— Improving heart health: Laughter has been shown to lower blood pressure, improve circulation, and reduce the risk of heart disease.

— Enhancing mood: Laughter can help to reduce anxiety and depression, improve self-esteem, and promote feelings of happiness and well-being.

— Strengthening relationships: Laughter is a powerful social bonding tool that can help to build stronger relationships and create a sense of community.

21: THE POWER OF LAUGHTER: FINDING JOY AND HUMOR IN LIFE

Finding Humor in Life

One of the biggest challenges in life is learning to find humor in even the most challenging situations. When we are faced with adversity or stress, it can be easy to get bogged down in negative emotions and lose our sense of humor.

However, by learning to see the funny side of life, we can reduce stress, improve our mood, and build resilience. Here are some tips for finding humor in life:

Look for the funny side: Try to find humor in everyday situations, even when things don't go as planned. Look for the absurd, the ironic, and the unexpected. By learning to see the humor in life, we can reduce stress and improve our mood.

Laugh at yourself: Don't take yourself too seriously. Learn to laugh at your mistakes and shortcomings. By learning to laugh at ourselves, we can reduce anxiety and improve our self-esteem.

Surround yourself with humor: Watch funny movies, read humorous books, and surround yourself with people who have a good sense of humor. By immersing ourselves in humor, we can improve our mood and reduce stress.

Practice gratitude: Gratitude is a powerful tool for improving our mood and reducing stress. By focusing on the positive aspects of life, we can find humor even in challenging situations.

Keep things in perspective: When faced with difficult situations, try to keep things in perspective. Ask yourself, "Will this matter in five years?" By learning to keep things in perspective, we can reduce stress and find humor in even the most challenging situations.

Incorporating Laughter into Daily Life

Incorporating more laughter and humor into our daily lives is essential for our physical, emotional, and mental well-being. Here are some practical tips for incorporating more laughter into your daily life:

Spend time with friends and family: Laughter is contagious. Spend time with friends and family who have a good sense of humor and enjoy making you laugh. This will not only improve your mood but also strengthen your relationships.

Watch comedy shows and movies: There is no shortage of comedy shows and movies to choose from. Find ones that resonate with your sense of humor and make you laugh out loud. This is an easy and enjoyable way to incorporate laughter into your daily routine.

Read humorous books: Reading humorous books is a great way to reduce stress and improve your mood. Find books by authors who make you laugh and set aside time each day to read.

Practice laughing exercises: There are laughing exercises and yoga classes that incorporate laughter as a form of therapy. These exercises can be done alone or in a group setting and are a fun way to boost your mood.

Practice self-compassion: Being kind to yourself and practicing self-compassion can help you find humor in difficult situations. When you make a mistake or have a setback, try to see the humor in it and be kind to yourself.

Find joy in the little things: Laughter doesn't have to be

complicated or forced. Find joy in the little things in life, like a funny meme, a silly joke, or a playful moment with your pet. By finding humor in the everyday, you can improve your mood and reduce stress.

Conclusion

Laughter is a powerful tool for improving our physical, emotional, and mental well-being. It has the power to transform our lives, heal our bodies and minds, and make us happier, healthier, and more resilient.

By learning to find humor in everyday situations, practicing self-compassion, and incorporating laughter into our daily routine, we can improve our mood, reduce stress, and live a happier, more fulfilling life.

So go ahead, laugh out loud, and discover the transformative power of true happiness.

22: Positive Relationships: Strengthening Your Connections with Others

As social creatures, humans thrive on positive relationships. Our connections with others are essential to our overall wellbeing and happiness. Positive relationships provide us with support, love, and a sense of belonging. They help us navigate life's challenges and celebrate its joys. In this chapter, we will explore the transformative power of positive relationships and discover practical strategies for strengthening our connections with others.

The Importance of Positive Relationships

Positive relationships are essential to our mental, emotional, and physical health. Studies have shown that people who have strong, positive relationships with others are happier, healthier, and more successful than those who are socially isolated. Positive relationships provide us with a sense of purpose, meaning, and belonging. They help us cope with stress and adversity and provide us with a support system to lean on when times get tough.

Positive relationships also have a significant impact on our brain chemistry. When we connect with others, our brains release a hormone called oxytocin, which is often referred to as the "love hormone." Oxytocin helps us feel bonded to others and promotes feelings of trust, empathy, and compassion. It also helps reduce stress and anxiety and promotes a sense of calm and wellbeing.

Positive relationships can also help us live longer. Studies have shown that people who have strong, positive relationships with others tend to live longer than those who are socially isolated. This may be because positive relationships provide us with emotional support and encourage us to take care of our physical health.

Building Positive Relationships

Building positive relationships takes time, effort, and commitment. It requires us to be vulnerable, open, and willing to connect with others. Here are some strategies for building positive relationships:

Be Authentic: Authenticity is key to building positive relationships. When we are authentic, we are true to ourselves and our values. This helps others feel more comfortable around us and encourages them to be authentic as well. Authenticity also helps build trust and promotes deeper connections with others.

Listen: Listening is an essential component of building positive relationships. When we listen to others, we show them that we value and respect their thoughts and feelings. This helps build trust and strengthens our connections with others. Listening also helps us learn about others and understand their perspectives, which can help us build more meaningful relationships.

Show Empathy: Empathy is the ability to understand and share the feelings of others. When we show empathy, we demonstrate that we care about others and are willing to support them. This helps build trust and promotes deeper connections with others.

Be Positive: Positive people attract positive relationships. When we approach others with a positive attitude, we are more likely to build positive relationships. Positivity also helps us cope with stress and adversity, which can help us build stronger connections with others.

22: POSITIVE RELATIONSHIPS: STRENGTHENING YOUR CONNECTIONS WITH OTHERS

Practice Gratitude: Gratitude is the practice of being thankful for what we have. When we practice gratitude, we focus on the positive aspects of our lives and appreciate the people who are important to us. This helps us build stronger connections with others and promotes feelings of happiness and contentment.

Maintaining Positive Relationships

Maintaining positive relationships requires ongoing effort and attention. Here are some strategies for maintaining positive relationships:

Communicate: Communication is essential to maintaining positive relationships. When we communicate with others, we show them that we value and care about them. Communication also helps us resolve conflicts and strengthen our connections with others.

Be Supportive: Supporting others is an essential component of maintaining positive relationships. When we support others, we demonstrate that we care about them and are willing to help them when they need it. This helps build trust and strengthens our connections with others.

22: POSITIVE RELATIONSHIPS: STRENGTHENING YOUR CONNECTIONS WITH OTHERS

Be Reliable: Reliability is key to maintaining positive relationships. When we are reliable, we demonstrate that we can be counted on and that we value our connections with others. Being reliable means following through on commitments, being on time, and being consistent in our behavior. This helps build trust and strengthens our connections with others.

Show Appreciation: Showing appreciation is important in maintaining positive relationships. When we show appreciation for others, we demonstrate that we value them and are grateful for their presence in our lives. This helps build stronger connections and promotes feelings of happiness and contentment.

Practice Forgiveness: Forgiveness is essential in maintaining positive relationships. When we forgive others, we let go of resentment and anger, and we allow ourselves to move forward. Forgiveness helps us heal from past hurts and strengthens our connections with others.

Challenges in Building Positive Relationships

Building positive relationships is not always easy. There are challenges that can arise, such as conflicts, disagreements, and misunderstandings. Here are some strategies for navigating these challenges:

Be Open: Being open to others' perspectives is important in navigating conflicts and disagreements. When we are open, we are more likely to find common ground and reach a resolution.

Communicate: Communication is essential in navigating conflicts and disagreements. When we communicate with others, we can clarify misunderstandings and work towards a resolution.

Practice Empathy: Practicing empathy can help us navigate conflicts and disagreements. When we try to understand others' perspectives, we are more likely to find common ground and reach a resolution.

Take Responsibility: Taking responsibility for our actions and behaviors is important in navigating conflicts and disagreements. When we take responsibility, we demonstrate that we value our connections with others and are willing to work towards a resolution.

Seek Help: Sometimes, navigating conflicts and disagreements requires the help of a professional, such as a therapist or mediator. Seeking help when needed can help us navigate challenging situations and maintain positive relationships.

Conclusion

Positive relationships are essential to our overall wellbeing and happiness. They provide us with support, love, and a sense of belonging. Building and maintaining positive relationships takes time, effort, and commitment, but the benefits are worth it. By being authentic, listening, showing empathy, being positive, and practicing gratitude, we can build stronger connections with others. By communicating, being supportive, being reliable, showing appreciation, and practicing forgiveness, we can maintain positive relationships. When challenges arise, being open, communicating, practicing empathy, taking responsibility, and seeking help can help us navigate conflicts and disagreements. By prioritizing positive relationships, we can unlock the transformative power of true happiness and live our best lives yet.

23: Communication: Building Healthy and Supportive Relationships

Communication is the cornerstone of all healthy and supportive relationships. Whether it be in personal or professional settings, the way we communicate with others can significantly impact the quality of our relationships and our overall happiness. In this chapter, we will explore the importance of effective communication and provide you with practical strategies to improve your communication skills and build stronger relationships.

The Power of Communication

Communication is the process of exchanging information, thoughts, and ideas between individuals or groups. It is a fundamental human need that helps us understand and connect with others. Effective communication involves not only the transmission of information but also the ability to listen actively and respond appropriately.

In personal relationships, communication is the foundation of trust, intimacy, and emotional support. The ability to express ourselves honestly and listen to others with empathy can deepen our connections with loved ones and enhance our overall wellbeing. In professional settings, effective communication is crucial for building successful partnerships, achieving common goals, and resolving conflicts.

On the other hand, poor communication can lead to misunderstandings, frustration, and even conflict. It can strain relationships and negatively impact our mental and emotional health. Therefore, it is essential to develop strong communication skills to improve the quality of our relationships and our overall happiness.

Effective Communication Strategies

Active Listening

Active listening involves giving our full attention to the speaker, focusing on their words and body language, and seeking to understand their perspective. It requires us to set aside our own thoughts and emotions and remain present in the moment.

To practice active listening, begin by making eye contact and nodding to show that you are engaged. Avoid interrupting the speaker and try to resist the urge to formulate a response before they finish speaking. Once they have finished, paraphrase what they said to ensure that you have understood their message correctly.

Expressing Yourself Clearly

Effective communication involves expressing yourself clearly and concisely. Be mindful of your tone of voice, body language, and choice of words. Speak in a calm and respectful manner, and avoid using inflammatory language or personal attacks.

When expressing your thoughts or feelings, be specific and provide examples to help the listener understand your perspective. If you are having difficulty expressing yourself, take a moment to collect your thoughts before continuing the conversation.

Empathy and Understanding

Empathy involves the ability to understand and share the feelings of another person. It is a crucial aspect of effective communication, particularly in personal relationships.

When we show empathy, we demonstrate that we value and respect the other person's emotions.

To practice empathy, put yourself in the other person's shoes and try to understand their perspective. Listen to their concerns without judgment and acknowledge their feelings. Ask questions to clarify their position and show that you are genuinely interested in understanding their point of view.

Non-Verbal Communication

Non-verbal communication involves the use of body language, gestures, and facial expressions to convey messages. It is an essential aspect of effective communication, particularly in personal relationships. Non-verbal cues can provide insight into a person's emotions and can help us better understand their perspective.

To improve your non-verbal communication, pay attention to your body language and facial expressions. Be aware of how your gestures and posture can affect the message you are trying to convey. Use eye contact to show that you are engaged in the conversation and open to the other person's perspective.

Active Feedback

Active feedback involves providing constructive feedback to the other person. It is an essential aspect of effective communication, particularly in professional settings. Feedback can help us identify areas for improvement and can lead to personal and professional growth.

When providing feedback, be specific and provide examples of the behavior or performance you are addressing. Use a calm and respectful tone of voice, and avoid personal attacks or judgment. Focus on the behavior or performance, not the person, and provide actionable suggestions for improvement.

Conflict Resolution

Conflict is an inevitable part of all relationships. Effective communication involves the ability to resolve conflicts in a constructive and respectful manner. When conflict arises, it is essential to remain calm and focus on finding a solution that works for both parties.

23: COMMUNICATION: BUILDING HEALTHY AND SUP-PORTIVE RELATIONSHIPS

To resolve conflicts effectively, begin by acknowledging the other person's perspective and expressing your own. Use active listening and empathy to understand each other's position. Brainstorm possible solutions together and find a compromise that meets both parties' needs.

Boundaries

Effective communication also involves setting and respecting boundaries. Boundaries are essential in all relationships, as they help us maintain our individuality and prevent us from being taken advantage of or mistreated.

To set boundaries, clearly communicate your needs and expectations to the other person. Be respectful but firm in expressing your boundaries. If your boundaries are not respected, consider limiting your interaction with the person or seeking outside support.

In conclusion, effective communication is crucial for building healthy and supportive relationships. By practicing active listening, expressing yourself clearly, showing empathy and understanding, improving your non-verbal communication, providing active feedback, resolving conflicts constructively, and setting boundaries, you can improve the quality of your relationships and enhance your overall happiness. Remember that communication is a skill that can be developed and improved over time. With practice and patience, you can become a better communicator and build stronger, more fulfilling relationships.

24: Romantic Love: Navigating Relationships and Finding Happiness in Love

Romantic love is a complex and multifaceted topic, one that has fascinated humans for centuries. Whether we're searching for it, experiencing it, or trying to make sense of it, love has the power to shape our lives in profound ways. In this chapter, we'll explore the many facets of romantic love and how it relates to our happiness and well-being.

The Nature of Romantic Love

At its core, romantic love is a deep and intense emotional connection between two people. It's a feeling of intimacy, passion, and vulnerability that can be both exhilarating and terrifying. When we're in love, we often feel a sense of completeness or wholeness, as if we've found our missing half. This intense connection can be a powerful source of happiness and fulfillment, but it can also be a source of pain and heartache when things don't work out.

One of the challenges of romantic love is that it's often accompanied by intense physical and emotional sensations that can cloud our judgment and make it difficult to think clearly. When we're in love, our brains release a flood of neurotransmitters, including dopamine, oxytocin, and serotonin, that can create a sense of euphoria and pleasure. This chemical cocktail can make it difficult to see our partner's flaws or make rational decisions about our relationship.

Navigating Relationships

Navigating a romantic relationship can be a challenging and rewarding experience. Whether you're just starting out or you've been together for years, building a healthy and fulfilling relationship requires effort and commitment from both partners. Here are some strategies for navigating relationships and finding happiness in love:

Communication: One of the most important aspects of any relationship is communication. Being able to express your thoughts, feelings, and needs in a clear and respectful way is essential for building trust and intimacy. Make sure you're taking the time to listen to your partner and respond with empathy and understanding.

Boundaries: Setting clear boundaries is important for maintaining a healthy relationship. This means communicating your limits and expectations and respecting your partner's boundaries as well. Boundaries can help prevent misunderstandings and conflicts and can also help build trust and respect in the relationship.

Conflict resolution: Conflict is a natural part of any relationship, but it's how you handle it that matters. Learning how to resolve conflicts in a constructive and respectful way is essential for building a strong and lasting relationship. This means avoiding blame and criticism, actively listening to your partner's perspective, and working together to find a solution that works for both of you.

Self-care: Taking care of yourself is essential for maintaining a healthy relationship. This means prioritizing your own needs and hobbies, spending time with friends and family, and practicing self-care activities like exercise, meditation, or journaling. When you feel fulfilled and happy on your own, you'll be better equipped to bring your best self to the relationship.

Finding Happiness in Love

While romantic love can be a powerful source of happiness

and fulfillment, it's important to remember that it's not the only source. Happiness is a multifaceted and complex emotion that can come from a variety of sources, including friendships, hobbies, and meaningful work. Here are some strategies for finding happiness in love:

Focus on the present moment: One of the biggest obstacles to happiness is worrying about the future or dwelling on the past. By focusing on the present moment and savoring the positive experiences in your relationship, you can cultivate a sense of gratitude and joy.

Cultivate self-love: Learning to love and accept yourself is essential for finding happiness in love. When you feel confident and comfortable in your own skin, you'll be better able to bring your best self to the relationship.

Practice gratitude: Gratitude is a powerful emotion that can help cultivate happiness and contentment in your relationship. By taking the time to appreciate the positive aspects of your partner and your relationship, you'll be more likely to feel fulfilled and satisfied.

Pursue common interests: Pursuing common interests and

hobbies with your partner is a great way to build a sense of shared purpose and connection. Whether it's hiking, cooking, or watching movies, finding activities that you both enjoy can help deepen your bond and bring you closer together.

Give back: Volunteering or engaging in acts of kindness with your partner can be a powerful way to experience happiness and fulfillment. By giving back to your community or supporting a cause you both care about, you'll be able to deepen your connection while also making a positive impact in the world.

Overcoming Adversity

While romantic love can be a powerful source of happiness and fulfillment, it can also be a source of pain and adversity. Whether it's dealing with infidelity, communication issues, or other challenges, overcoming adversity in a relationship can be a difficult and painful process. Here are some strategies for overcoming adversity and finding happiness in love:

Seek support: When dealing with adversity in a relationship, it's important to seek support from friends, family, or a therapist. Having someone to talk to and offer support can help you navigate difficult emotions and find a path forward.

Practice forgiveness: Forgiveness is a powerful tool for overcoming adversity in a relationship. By choosing to forgive your partner and let go of past hurts, you'll be able to move forward and rebuild trust and intimacy.

Take responsibility: It's important to take responsibility for your own actions and behavior in a relationship. By owning up to your mistakes and making an effort to change, you'll be able to create a more positive and healthy dynamic with your partner.

Focus on the positive: When dealing with adversity in a relationship, it's important to focus on the positive aspects of your partner and your relationship. By cultivating gratitude and appreciation for the good things in your life, you'll be more likely to find happiness and fulfillment in your relationship.

Conclusion

24: ROMANTIC LOVE: NAVIGATING RELATIONSHIPS AND FINDING HAPPINESS IN LOVE

Romantic love is a complex and multifaceted topic, one that has the power to shape our lives in profound ways. Whether we're navigating a new relationship, trying to find happiness in love, or overcoming adversity, there are many strategies and tips we can use to cultivate a more positive and fulfilling relationship. By focusing on communication, boundaries, conflict resolution, self-care, gratitude, and forgiveness, we can build strong and lasting relationships that bring us happiness, fulfillment, and a sense of purpose in life.

25: Family and Happiness: Balancing Family Life and Personal Goals

Family is one of the most important parts of our lives. It provides us with love, support, and a sense of belonging. It is where we learn our values and build our relationships. However, family life can also be challenging and can sometimes interfere with our personal goals and happiness. In this chapter, we will explore how to balance family life and personal goals in order to achieve true happiness.

Firstly, it is important to understand that family and personal goals are not mutually exclusive. It is possible to have a happy family life while pursuing your personal goals. However, it does require some effort and balance. One of the most important things is to have open communication with your family members. Talk to your spouse, children, or other family members about your personal goals and aspirations. Explain how these goals can benefit the family as a whole and ask for their support. This can help to avoid any misunderstandings or conflicts that may arise.

Another important factor is time management. Balancing

family life and personal goals requires careful planning and organization. It is important to prioritize your time and schedule accordingly. Make a schedule that includes time for family activities, work, and personal pursuits. This can help to ensure that you have enough time for everything that is important to you.

In addition, it is important to set realistic goals. Setting unrealistic goals can lead to disappointment and frustration, which can ultimately affect your family life. Make sure that your personal goals are achievable and do not require sacrificing your family life. This can help to ensure that you are able to maintain a healthy balance between your personal goals and your family life.

One of the key aspects of balancing family life and personal goals is finding ways to integrate the two. Look for opportunities to involve your family in your personal pursuits. For example, if you are interested in fitness, consider taking your family to the gym with you or going for a family bike ride. This can help to promote a healthy lifestyle for everyone and can also provide quality time together.

It is also important to make time for your family. While pur-

suing your personal goals is important, it is equally important to spend quality time with your family. Make time for
family activities such as game nights, movie nights, or weekend trips. This can help to strengthen your family relationships and create lasting memories.

In addition to spending time with your family, it is important to prioritize self-care. Taking care of yourself is essential
to achieving true happiness. Make sure to take time for
activities that you enjoy, such as reading, practicing yoga, or
taking a relaxing bath. This can help to reduce stress and
improve your overall well-being, which can ultimately benefit your family as well.

Finally, it is important to be flexible and adaptable. Life is
unpredictable, and it is important to be able to adjust to
changes as they occur. Sometimes, family responsibilities
may require you to put your personal goals on hold temporarily. In these situations, it is important to be patient and
understanding, and to remember that your personal goals
can still be achieved in the future.

Balancing family life and personal goals is not always easy,
but it is possible with effort and commitment. By prioritiz-

ing communication, time management, realistic goal-setting, integration, self-care, and flexibility, you can achieve true happiness while maintaining a healthy and fulfilling family life. Remember, the key to happiness is finding balance in all areas of your life.

26: Work-Life Balance: Finding Harmony in Your Career and Personal Life

In today's fast-paced and competitive world, finding work-life balance has become increasingly important for achieving happiness and well-being. Many people struggle to balance the demands of their career with their personal life, leading to stress, burnout, and a lack of fulfillment. In this chapter, we will explore how to find harmony between your career and personal life to achieve true happiness.

Firstly, it is important to understand what work-life balance means. Work-life balance refers to the ability to manage the demands of work and personal life in a way that allows you to fulfill your responsibilities and achieve your goals in both areas. It is not about achieving perfect balance between the two, but rather finding a harmony that works for you.

One of the most important factors in achieving work-life balance is setting priorities. Determine what is most important to you in both your career and personal life. This can help you to identify where you need to focus your time and energy. Make a list of your top priorities in each area and use this as a guide for making decisions about how to spend your time.

Another important factor is time management. Effective time management can help you to balance the demands of work and personal life. Make a schedule that includes time for work, personal pursuits, and self-care. Prioritize your time and avoid over-committing yourself. This can help to ensure that you have enough time for everything that is important to you.

In addition, it is important to set boundaries. This means establishing clear limits between your work and personal life. For example, avoid checking work emails or taking phone calls during your personal time. Similarly, avoid personal distractions during work hours. This can help you to maintain a healthy balance between the two.

One of the key aspects of achieving work-life balance is finding meaning and fulfillment in both your career and personal life. This requires aligning your career with your personal values and interests. Consider what motivates you and what gives you a sense of purpose in both areas. Look for ways to integrate your personal passions into your career and vice versa.

It is also important to prioritize self-care. Taking care of
yourself is essential to achieving work-life balance. Make
time for activities that you enjoy, such as exercise, reading,
or spending time with loved ones. This can help to reduce
stress and improve your overall well-being, which can ultimately benefit both your career and personal life.

Another important factor is support. Surround yourself with
a supportive network of friends, family, and colleagues.
Seek out mentors or coaches who can provide guidance and
advice. This can help you to navigate the challenges of both
your career and personal life.

Finally, it is important to be flexible and adaptable. Life is
unpredictable, and it is important to be able to adjust to
changes as they occur. Sometimes, work or personal responsibilities may require you to put other things on hold
temporarily. In these situations, it is important to be patient
and understanding, and to remember that you can still
achieve your goals in the future.

Achieving work-life balance is not always easy, but it is possible with effort and commitment. By setting priorities, managing your time effectively, setting boundaries, finding meaning and fulfillment, prioritizing self-care, seeking support, and being flexible, you can find harmony between your career and personal life and achieve true happiness. Remember, the key to happiness is finding balance in all areas of your life.

27: Money and Happiness: Understanding the Relationship Between Wealth and Well-Being

Money and happiness are two of the most fundamental concepts in our lives. We often hear the saying that money can't buy happiness, but is that really true? Does wealth have a significant impact on our overall well-being, or is it just a myth perpetuated by society? In this chapter, we'll explore the complex relationship between money and happiness and provide some strategies for achieving both.

The Relationship Between Money and Happiness

Studies have shown that money and happiness are indeed connected, but the relationship is not as straightforward as we might think. While it's true that having enough money to meet our basic needs and some of our wants can contribute to our happiness, beyond a certain point, additional wealth doesn't necessarily lead to greater well-being.

In fact, studies have found that once we have enough money to live comfortably and meet our basic needs, additional income doesn't have a significant impact on our happiness levels. This is known as the "happiness plateau," and it suggests that beyond a certain level of income, we are no longer motivated by the pursuit of more money and material possessions.

Furthermore, studies have found that people who prioritize money and material possessions are often less happy than those who prioritize other values, such as relationships, personal growth, and helping others. This suggests that the pursuit of wealth and material possessions can actually detract from our overall well-being.

So, while money can contribute to our happiness to a certain extent, it's important to keep in mind that there are other factors that are much more important for our overall well-being.

Strategies for Achieving Money and Happiness

If you're looking to achieve both money and happiness, here are some strategies to consider:

Define your priorities: Before you can achieve both money and happiness, it's important to understand what you truly value in life. Take some time to reflect on what's most important to you, whether it's relationships, personal growth, financial stability, or something else entirely.

Live within your means: While having more money can contribute to our happiness to a certain extent, living beyond our means can have the opposite effect. Make sure you're living within your means and avoid taking on excessive debt or overspending on things that don't truly matter to you.

Prioritize experiences over material possessions: Studies have found that experiences, such as travel, hobbies, and spending time with loved ones, can contribute more to our happiness than material possessions. Prioritize experiences over material possessions whenever possible.

Cultivate gratitude: Practicing gratitude can help us appreciate what we already have and avoid getting caught up in the pursuit of more. Take some time each day to reflect on what you're grateful for, whether it's your health, your relationships, or something else entirely.

Give back: Helping others can be a powerful source of happiness and fulfillment. Look for ways to give back to your community, whether it's through volunteering, donating to charity, or simply being kind to those around you.

Invest in your personal growth: Investing in your personal growth can help you achieve both money and happiness. Consider taking courses or pursuing certifications that can help you advance in your career, or explore hobbies and interests that bring you joy and fulfillment.

Practice mindfulness: Practicing mindfulness can help you stay present in the moment and avoid getting caught up in worries about the future or regrets about the past. Consider incorporating mindfulness practices, such as meditation or yoga, into your daily routine.

Conclusion

Money and happiness are undoubtedly connected, but the relationship is much more complex than we might think. While having enough money to meet our basic needs can contribute to our happiness, beyond a certain point, additional wealth doesn't necessarily lead to greater well-being.

If you're looking to achieve both money and happiness, it's important to define your priorities, live within your means, prioritize experiences over material possessions, cultivate gratitude, give back, invest in your personal growth, and practice mindfulness.

Ultimately, achieving true happiness requires a holistic approach that goes beyond just accumulating wealth and material possessions. It requires us to prioritize our relationships, personal growth, and values, and to stay present in the moment, appreciating what we have and giving back to others.

By focusing on these strategies and cultivating a mindset of gratitude and mindfulness, we can achieve both money and happiness in our lives. It's up to us to define what true happiness means to us and to take action towards achieving it, one step at a time.

28: Living in the Present: Letting Go of Regret and Anxiety

As humans, we have a natural tendency to dwell on the past or worry about the future. We often find ourselves regretting the choices we made or feeling anxious about the things that might happen. However, living in the present moment is essential to achieving true happiness and inner peace.

The present moment is all we have, and it's essential to embrace it fully. When we live in the past or worry about the future, we miss out on the present moment, and we miss out on life. The key to living in the present is to let go of regret and anxiety and focus on what's happening right now.

Letting go of regret is easier said than done, but it's necessary for achieving happiness. Regret is a powerful emotion that can hold us back from moving forward in life. We may regret things we did or didn't do, opportunities we missed, or relationships we didn't pursue. However, holding onto regret does not change the past. Instead, it keeps us stuck in a cycle of negative thinking that can affect our present and future.

To let go of regret, we must first acknowledge it. It's essential to recognize the feelings of sadness, disappointment, or anger that come with regret. Once we've acknowledged our regret, we can start to work on letting it go. One way to do this is to forgive ourselves for the mistakes we've made. We're all human, and we all make mistakes. Forgiving ourselves allows us to move forward without the weight of regret holding us down.

Another way to let go of regret is to learn from our mistakes. Mistakes can be valuable learning experiences that can help us grow and develop as individuals. By recognizing what we did wrong, we can avoid making the same mistakes in the future. This can give us a sense of empowerment and control over our lives.

In addition to letting go of regret, it's also essential to let go of anxiety. Anxiety is a natural response to uncertainty, but it can also be a source of great distress. Anxiety can keep us from living in the present moment and enjoying life to the fullest.

To let go of anxiety, we must first identify the source of our worries. What is causing us to feel anxious? Is it something we can control, or is it out of our hands? Once we've identified the source of our anxiety, we can start to work on managing it.

One way to manage anxiety is to practice mindfulness. Mindfulness is the practice of being fully present in the moment, without judgment. When we're mindful, we're not dwelling on the past or worrying about the future. Instead, we're focused on what's happening right now. This can help us reduce anxiety and stress, and increase our sense of calm and well-being.

Another way to manage anxiety is to take action. If there's something we can do to address our worries, we should take action. For example, if we're worried about our health, we can make an appointment with our doctor. If we're worried about our finances, we can create a budget and start saving. Taking action can give us a sense of control over our lives and reduce our anxiety.

Living in the present moment is not always easy, but it's essential for achieving happiness and inner peace. By letting go of regret and anxiety, we can focus on what's happening right now and enjoy life to the fullest. We can't change the past, and we can't predict the future, but we can control how we respond to the present moment. By living in the present, we can create a fulfilling life that is full of joy, meaning, and purpose.

29: Overcoming Obstacles: The Importance of Resilience in Achieving Happiness

Life is full of obstacles, challenges, and setbacks that can throw us off course, leaving us feeling lost, confused, and even defeated. Whether it's a difficult job, a toxic relationship, or a health issue, we all face challenges that can test our resilience and our ability to overcome adversity. But despite the challenges that we face, happiness is still within our reach. It's not just about having a positive outlook or a cheerful disposition, but it's about developing the resilience and inner strength to weather life's storms and come out stronger on the other side.

Resilience is the ability to adapt and cope with stress, adversity, and change. It's not just about bouncing back from difficult situations, but it's about using those experiences to grow and become stronger. Resilience is a vital component of happiness because it helps us navigate life's challenges with grace, strength, and determination. Resilience is not something that we are born with, but it's a skill that we can develop through practice, self-reflection, and perseverance.

29: OVERCOMING OBSTACLES: THE IMPORTANCE OF RESILIENCE IN ACHIEVING HAPPINESS

There are several ways to build resilience and overcome obstacles. The first step is to accept that challenges are a natural part of life. We cannot control everything that happens to us, but we can control how we react to it. It's essential to adopt a growth mindset and see challenges as opportunities for growth and learning. Instead of feeling defeated, we can view obstacles as a chance to build resilience and develop new skills. By embracing challenges and learning from them, we can become more resilient and better equipped to handle whatever life throws our way.

Another key factor in building resilience is social support. Humans are social creatures, and we need to feel connected to others to thrive. When we face difficult times, having a supportive network of friends, family, and mentors can make all the difference. Social support can provide us with a sounding board, advice, and encouragement. It can help us feel less alone and more empowered to overcome obstacles. Developing strong relationships with others can help us build resilience and find happiness even in the face of adversity.

Mindfulness is also an essential tool for building resilience.

29: OVERCOMING OBSTACLES: THE IMPORTANCE OF RESILIENCE IN ACHIEVING HAPPINESS

Mindfulness is the practice of being present in the moment and accepting things as they are without judgment. It helps us cultivate awareness and compassion for ourselves and others. Mindfulness can help us manage stress and anxiety and build our resilience by enabling us to stay grounded and centered during challenging times. Practicing mindfulness regularly can help us cultivate a sense of calm, clarity, and focus that can help us overcome obstacles and find happiness even in difficult times.

Finally, developing a sense of purpose and meaning in life can help us build resilience and find happiness. Purpose and meaning give us direction and motivation to overcome obstacles and navigate challenging times. They help us stay focused on what is important and give us a sense of fulfillment and satisfaction. By aligning our values, goals, and actions, we can cultivate a sense of purpose and meaning that can sustain us through difficult times and help us find happiness even in the face of adversity.

In conclusion, happiness is not just about having a positive attitude or a cheerful disposition. It's about developing resilience and inner strength to navigate life's challenges with

29: OVERCOMING OBSTACLES: THE IMPORTANCE OF RESILIENCE IN ACHIEVING HAPPINESS

grace, determination, and perseverance. Resilience is a vital component of happiness because it helps us overcome obstacles, adapt to change, and grow into our best selves. By adopting a growth mindset, building social support, practicing mindfulness, and cultivating a sense of purpose and meaning, we can build resilience and find lasting happiness even in the face of adversity.

30: Finding Happiness in Diversity: Celebrating Differences and Embracing Inclusion

Happiness is a state of mind that is often associated with feelings of contentment, joy, and satisfaction. It is something that we all aspire to have in our lives. However, achieving true happiness can be elusive and challenging, especially in today's world, where there are so many distractions and pressures.

One of the keys to finding happiness is to embrace diversity and celebrate differences. In a world that is becoming increasingly polarized, it is more important than ever to recognize that every person is unique and has something valuable to contribute to society. By embracing diversity, we can create a more inclusive and compassionate world where everyone feels valued and accepted.

But what does it mean to embrace diversity? At its core, it means recognizing and respecting the differences that exist among individuals and communities. It means acknowledging that people come from different backgrounds, cultures, and experiences, and that these differences should be celebrated, not feared or judged.

One way to embrace diversity is to cultivate an attitude of curiosity and openness. This means being willing to learn about other cultures, beliefs, and ways of life. It means asking questions and seeking to understand the perspectives of others. By doing so, we can broaden our own horizons and gain a deeper appreciation for the richness and diversity of the world around us.

Another way to embrace diversity is to actively seek out opportunities to connect with people from different backgrounds. This can be done through volunteering, attending cultural events, or joining community groups that are dedicated to promoting diversity and inclusion. By building relationships with people who are different from us, we can gain a deeper understanding of their experiences and perspectives, and in turn, become more empathetic and compassionate.

Of course, embracing diversity is not always easy. It requires us to confront our own biases and prejudices, and to challenge the assumptions and stereotypes that we may hold. It also requires us to be willing to have difficult conversations and to listen to feedback from others.

But the rewards of embracing diversity are immense. By celebrating differences and promoting inclusion, we can create a more harmonious and peaceful world. We can also experience greater personal growth and fulfillment, as we learn from and connect with people who are different from us.

So how can we start embracing diversity in our own lives? Here are some practical tips:

– Be curious and open-minded: Approach new people and situations with a sense of curiosity and a willingness to learn.

– Challenge your assumptions: Be aware of your own biases and prejudices, and actively work to challenge them.

– Seek out diversity: Look for opportunities to connect with people from different backgrounds, whether it's through volunteer work, community events, or social media groups.

– Listen actively: When engaging with people from different backgrounds, listen actively and try to understand their perspectives without judgment.

30: FINDING HAPPINESS IN DIVERSITY: CELEBRAT-ING DIFFERENCES AND EMBRACING INCLUSION

– Practice empathy: Put yourself in the shoes of others and try to see the world from their point of view.

– Speak up against discrimination: When you witness discrimination or bias, speak up and take action to promote inclusion and acceptance.

By taking these steps, we can all play a role in promoting diversity and inclusion, and in creating a more harmonious and peaceful world. And in doing so, we can also find greater happiness and fulfillment in our own lives.

31: Inner Peace: Cultivating Serenity and Stillness in Your Life

The pursuit of happiness is a never-ending journey. It is a pursuit that requires a lot of effort, dedication, and most importantly, inner peace. Inner peace is the foundation upon which true happiness is built. Without inner peace, happiness becomes an elusive dream that is never fully realized. Inner peace is the calm, quiet, and stillness that lies within us, waiting to be discovered.

In today's fast-paced world, finding inner peace can be challenging. We are bombarded with constant distractions, pressures, and stresses that make it difficult to find a moment of stillness. We are always connected to technology, social media, and a never-ending to-do list. In the midst of all this chaos, finding inner peace may seem impossible.

However, cultivating serenity and stillness in our lives is essential for our well-being. Inner peace allows us to be present in the moment, to connect with ourselves and others, and to find joy in the simple things in life. In this chapter, we will explore the importance of inner peace and the strategies and practices that can help us cultivate it.

31: INNER PEACE: CULTIVATING SERENITY AND STILLNESS IN YOUR LIFE

What is Inner Peace?

Inner peace is a state of being that is characterized by calmness, tranquility, and a sense of well-being. It is the absence of turmoil, anxiety, and stress. Inner peace is not a permanent state, but rather a fleeting moment that can be experienced when we are present in the moment and fully connected with ourselves.

Inner peace is not something that can be acquired externally. It is not a product that can be purchased or a destination that can be reached. Inner peace is already within us. It is a natural state of being that we can tap into by quieting our minds and becoming present.

The Importance of Inner Peace

Inner peace is essential for our well-being. It allows us to connect with ourselves and others on a deeper level, to find joy in the simple things in life, and to navigate the challenges and pressures of everyday life with grace and ease.

When we are in a state of inner peace, we are better able to manage our emotions and reactions to external events. We are less likely to be reactive or impulsive and more likely to respond in a calm and measured way. Inner peace also allows us to be more resilient in the face of adversity, to bounce back from setbacks, and to find meaning and purpose in difficult times.

Strategies for Cultivating Inner Peace

Cultivating inner peace requires intention, effort, and practice. It is a skill that can be developed over time with the right strategies and techniques. Here are some strategies that can help you cultivate inner peace:

Mindfulness Meditation: Mindfulness meditation is a powerful tool for cultivating inner peace. It involves bringing your attention to the present moment, without judgment or distraction. By practicing mindfulness meditation regularly, you can train your mind to be more present and focused, and to let go of distractions and worries.

Yoga: Yoga is another powerful practice for cultivating inner peace. It combines physical postures with breathwork and meditation, creating a holistic approach to health and well-being. Yoga helps to quiet the mind, reduce stress and anxiety, and increase overall well-being.

Gratitude Practice: Gratitude is a powerful practice for cultivating inner peace. By focusing on the things in your life that you are grateful for, you can shift your perspective and cultivate a sense of contentment and joy. Practicing gratitude regularly can help you cultivate a sense of inner peace and well-being.

Journaling: Journaling is a powerful tool for self-reflection and self-awareness. By writing down your thoughts and feelings, you can gain insight into your inner world and cultivate a deeper sense of self-awareness. Journaling can help you process difficult emotions, reduce stress, and cultivate inner peace.

Mindful Breathing: Mindful breathing is a simple yet powerful practice for cultivating inner peace. By focusing your attention on your breath, you can quiet your mind, reduce stress, and cultivate a sense of calm and relaxation.

Nature Walks: Spending time in nature is a powerful way to cultivate inner peace. Nature has a way of slowing us down and helping us connect with the present moment. By taking a walk in nature, you can quiet your mind, reduce stress, and cultivate a sense of peace and tranquility.

Digital Detox: Our constant connection to technology can be a major source of stress and distraction. Taking a break from technology, even for a short time, can help you cultivate a sense of calm and stillness. Try turning off your phone for an hour or two each day, or taking a digital detox weekend to give yourself a break from the constant stimulation.

Self-Care: Taking care of yourself is essential for cultivating inner peace. Make time for activities that bring you joy, such as reading, listening to music, or taking a relaxing bath. Prioritize sleep, exercise, and healthy eating to support your overall well-being.

Incorporating these practices into your daily routine can help you cultivate a sense of inner peace and well-being. Remember that cultivating inner peace is a journey, not a destination. Be patient with yourself and trust the process.

Challenges to Cultivating Inner Peace

Cultivating inner peace can be challenging, especially in

today's fast-paced world. Here are some common challenges to cultivating inner peace and strategies for overcoming them:

Distractions: Distractions are everywhere, making it challenging to cultivate inner peace. Try setting boundaries around technology, scheduling time for mindfulness meditation or other practices, and creating a designated space for self-care activities.

Self-Doubt: Self-doubt can undermine your efforts to cultivate inner peace. Practice self-compassion and focus on your strengths and accomplishments. Surround yourself with supportive people who lift you up and believe in you.

Busy Schedule: A busy schedule can make it challenging to find time for self-care and mindfulness practices. Try scheduling time for these practices into your calendar, and prioritize them like any other important task.

Negative Thinking: Negative thinking can be a major barrier to cultivating inner peace. Challenge negative thoughts with positive affirmations, gratitude practices, and self-compassion. Surround yourself with positive people and uplifting media.

Stress: Stress is a major obstacle to inner peace. Practice stress-management techniques such as mindful breathing, yoga, and journaling to reduce stress and cultivate a sense of calm.

Conclusion

Cultivating inner peace is essential for our well-being and happiness. It allows us to be present in the moment, to connect with ourselves and others, and to navigate the challenges and pressures of everyday life with grace and ease. By incorporating mindfulness practices, self-care, and stress-management techniques into our daily routine, we can cultivate a sense of inner peace that will support us on our journey to happiness and fulfillment. Remember that cultivating inner peace is a journey, not a destination. Be patient with yourself, trust the process, and enjoy the journey.

32: Personal Growth: Continuously Improving Yourself for Lasting Happiness

Introduction:

Personal growth is an essential component of living a fulfilling life. It involves improving yourself in various aspects of life, including your mental, emotional, physical, and spiritual well-being. Personal growth is not a one-time event but a continuous journey of self-discovery and self-improvement. In this chapter, we will explore the concept of personal growth and the importance of continuously improving yourself for lasting happiness. We will also provide you with proven strategies and practical tips that you can use to achieve personal growth and live your best life yet.

Understanding Personal Growth:

Personal growth is the process of improving oneself through self-awareness, self-discovery, and self-improvement. It involves identifying your strengths and weaknesses, setting goals, and taking actions to achieve those goals. Personal growth is not about perfection but about progress. It is about recognizing that you are not perfect, but you can always strive to become a better version of yourself.

Personal growth involves improving various aspects of your life, including your mental, emotional, physical, and spiritual well-being. It involves developing healthy habits, improving your relationships, enhancing your skills and knowledge, and finding a sense of purpose and meaning in life.

Importance of Personal Growth:

Personal growth is essential for several reasons. Firstly, it helps you to live a fulfilling life by enabling you to develop your potential and achieve your goals. It gives you a sense of purpose and meaning in life and helps you to feel more satisfied and contented.

Secondly, personal growth helps you to improve your relationships with others. When you develop self-awareness and emotional intelligence, you become better equipped to handle conflicts and communicate effectively with others. This, in turn, leads to stronger and more meaningful relationships.

Thirdly, personal growth helps you to develop resilience and cope better with adversity. When you continuously work on improving yourself, you become more adaptable and better able to handle challenges and setbacks in life.

Strategies for Achieving Personal Growth:

Develop Self-Awareness:

Self-awareness is the foundation of personal growth. It involves understanding your thoughts, emotions, and behaviors and how they impact your life. You can develop self-awareness by practicing mindfulness, journaling, and seeking feedback from others.

Set Goals:

Setting goals is essential for personal growth. It gives you a sense of direction and helps you to focus your energy and resources on achieving what is important to you. When setting goals, make sure they are specific, measurable, achievable, relevant, and time-bound.

Learn Continuously:

Continuous learning is crucial for personal growth. It involves seeking new knowledge, skills, and experiences that enable you to become a better version of yourself. You can learn through reading books, attending courses, and seeking mentorship.

Practice Gratitude:

Gratitude is an essential aspect of personal growth. It involves focusing on the positive aspects of your life and being thankful for them. Gratitude helps you to cultivate a positive mindset, which, in turn, leads to greater happiness and well-being.

Cultivate Healthy Habits:

Healthy habits are crucial for personal growth. They help you to maintain your physical and mental well-being, which is essential for achieving your goals and living a fulfilling life. Healthy habits include exercise, healthy eating, getting enough sleep, and managing stress.

Find Meaning and Purpose:

Finding meaning and purpose in life is essential for personal growth. It involves identifying your values, passions, and interests and aligning them with your goals and actions. When you find meaning and purpose in life, you become more motivated and inspired to achieve your goals and live a fulfilling life.

Practical Tips for Achieving Personal Growth:

Take small steps:

Personal growth is a journey that requires patience and consistency. Take small steps every day towards your goals and focus on making progress rather than achieving perfection overnight.

Embrace failures:

Failures are inevitable in life, and they provide valuable lessons that enable us to grow and improve. Instead of being discouraged by failures, embrace them as opportunities to learn and grow.

Surround yourself with positive influences:

The people you surround yourself with have a significant impact on your personal growth. Surround yourself with people who inspire and motivate you to become a better version of yourself.

Practice self-care:

Self-care is essential for personal growth. Take care of your physical, emotional, and mental well-being by practicing self-care activities such as meditation, yoga, or spending time in nature.

Practice forgiveness:

Forgiveness is a crucial aspect of personal growth. Let go of grudges and resentments towards others and yourself, and focus on moving forward with a positive mindset.

Celebrate your progress:

Take time to celebrate your progress and achievements, no matter how small. Celebrating your progress helps to keep you motivated and inspired to continue working towards your goals.

Conclusion:

32: PERSONAL GROWTH: CONTINUOUSLY IMPROVING YOURSELF FOR LASTING HAPPINESS

Personal growth is a continuous journey that requires commitment and effort. It involves improving various aspects of your life, including your mental, emotional, physical, and spiritual well-being. By developing self-awareness, setting goals, cultivating healthy habits, and finding meaning and purpose in life, you can achieve personal growth and live a fulfilling life. Remember to take small steps, embrace failures, surround yourself with positive influences, practice self-care, practice forgiveness, and celebrate your progress. With these strategies and tips, you can unlock the transformative power of true happiness and live your best life yet.

33: Habits for Happiness: Creating Daily Routines for a Fulfilling Life

As human beings, we are creatures of habit. Our daily routines and habits play a significant role in shaping the quality of our lives. In fact, research has shown that our habits can determine up to 40% of our daily actions, thoughts, and emotions. Therefore, it is no surprise that developing habits for happiness is an essential step towards achieving a fulfilling life.

Happiness is a state of mind that is influenced by our thoughts, feelings, and behaviors. Developing habits that foster positive thoughts, emotions, and behaviors can help us cultivate a lasting sense of happiness and well-being. In this chapter, we will explore some practical habits that you can develop to increase your happiness and create a fulfilling life.

Gratitude: Cultivate an Attitude of Gratitude

Gratitude is a powerful emotion that can help us shift our focus from what we lack to what we have. When we practice gratitude, we develop an attitude of appreciation for the things and people in our lives. This habit can help us develop a more positive outlook on life, which in turn can lead to greater happiness.

To cultivate an attitude of gratitude, start by keeping a gratitude journal. Each day, write down three things that you are grateful for. They can be as simple as the sun shining, a delicious cup of coffee, or a kind gesture from a friend. As you write, try to focus on the feeling of gratitude and appreciation that you experience. Over time, this habit can help you develop a more positive mindset and increase your overall sense of happiness.

Mindfulness: Practice Mindfulness Meditation

Mindfulness is the practice of being present in the moment and paying attention to our thoughts, feelings, and sensations without judgment. Mindfulness meditation is a powerful tool for developing mindfulness and increasing happiness. Research has shown that regular mindfulness meditation can help reduce stress, improve mood, and increase feelings of well-being.

To start practicing mindfulness meditation, find a quiet

place where you can sit comfortably for a few minutes. Close your eyes and focus on your breath. Notice the sensation of the air flowing in and out of your body. If your mind wanders, gently bring your attention back to your breath. Start with just a few minutes a day and gradually increase the duration of your practice over time. With regular practice, mindfulness meditation can become a habit that helps you cultivate a greater sense of happiness and inner peace.

Exercise: Move Your Body

Exercise is not only essential for physical health but also for mental health and well-being. Regular exercise has been shown to reduce stress, improve mood, and increase feelings of happiness. Developing a habit of regular exercise can be a powerful tool for increasing happiness and creating a fulfilling life.

To start an exercise habit, find an activity that you enjoy and can realistically incorporate into your daily routine. It could be as simple as taking a daily walk or trying a new fitness class. Start with a realistic goal, such as exercising for 30 minutes a day, and gradually increase the duration and intensity of your workouts over time. With regular exercise, you can improve your physical health and mental well-being, leading to greater happiness and fulfillment.

Connection: Nurture Your Relationships

Human beings are social creatures, and our relationships with others play a crucial role in our happiness and well-being. Developing a habit of nurturing our relationships can help us cultivate a greater sense of happiness and fulfillment in life.

To nurture your relationships, start by making time for the people in your life. Set aside time each week to connect with friends and family, whether it's through phone calls, video chats, or in-person meetings. Make an effort to show appreciation for the people in your life, whether it's through a kind gesture or a heartfelt compliment. By nurturing your relationships, you can create a sense of connection and belonging that can help you feel happier and more fulfilled in life.

Learning: Feed Your Mind

Learning is a lifelong process, and developing a habit of

continuous learning can help us expand our knowledge, skills, and perspectives. Engaging in learning activities can also increase feelings of fulfillment and happiness.

To develop a habit of continuous learning, start by identifying an area of interest or skill that you would like to develop. This could be anything from learning a new language to taking up a new hobby. Find resources such as books, courses, or online tutorials that can help you learn more about your chosen topic. Set aside time each day or week to engage in learning activities, and track your progress over time. By feeding your mind with new knowledge and skills, you can increase your sense of fulfillment and happiness.

Self-Care: Take Care of Yourself

Self-care is essential for our physical, mental, and emotional well-being. Developing a habit of self-care can help us prioritize our health and happiness, leading to a more fulfilling life.

To develop a habit of self-care, start by identifying activities that make you feel good and rejuvenated. This could be anything from taking a relaxing bath to practicing yoga or meditation. Make time for self-care activities each day or week and prioritize your health and well-being. By taking care of yourself, you can increase your happiness and overall sense of fulfillment.

Purpose: Find Your Why

Having a sense of purpose in life can give us direction and meaning, which in turn can lead to greater happiness and fulfillment. Finding your why can help you identify your passions, values, and goals, which can guide you towards a more fulfilling life.

To find your why, start by reflecting on your values, interests, and skills. Consider what brings you the most joy and fulfillment, and how you can use these to make a positive impact on the world. Set goals that align with your values and work towards achieving them. By finding your why and working towards your goals, you can create a sense of purpose and meaning in your life, leading to greater happiness and fulfillment.

In conclusion, developing habits for happiness is a crucial step towards achieving a fulfilling life. By cultivating habits such as gratitude, mindfulness, exercise, connection, learning, self-care, and purpose, we can increase our overall sense of well-being and happiness. Start by identifying one or two habits that resonate with you and make a commitment to incorporate them into your daily routine. With consistent effort and practice, these habits can become a natural part of your daily life, leading to a happier and more fulfilling existence.

34: Finding Balance: Creating a Sustainable Lifestyle for Long-Term Happiness

Happiness is a state of being that is often elusive, particularly in the fast-paced world we live in. We all want to be happy, but we often find ourselves caught up in the daily grind of work, family responsibilities, and social obligations. We may try to find happiness in material possessions, relationships, or external achievements, but these things can only provide temporary satisfaction.

True happiness comes from within, and it requires a balance between different areas of our lives. In this chapter, we will explore the importance of finding balance and creating a sustainable lifestyle for long-term happiness. We will discuss the different aspects of life that require balance, and we will provide practical tips and strategies for achieving this balance.

Work-Life Balance

One of the most important areas of life that requires balance is work. Many of us spend a significant portion of our lives at work, and it can be challenging to find a healthy balance between work and other aspects of life. Working long hours, taking on too many responsibilities, and neglecting our personal lives can lead to stress, burnout, and unhappiness.

To achieve work-life balance, it is essential to set clear boundaries and prioritize your time. You can start by establishing specific working hours and sticking to them, avoiding work-related tasks outside of these hours. It's also essential to prioritize your personal life and make time for hobbies, relationships, and self-care. Taking regular breaks throughout the day and unplugging from technology during non-work hours can also help you recharge and feel more balanced.

Physical Health and Well-Being

Another critical area of life that requires balance is physical health and well-being. Our bodies need proper care and attention to function at their best, and neglecting our physical health can lead to chronic health problems and decreased happiness.

To achieve balance in this area, it is crucial to prioritize healthy habits such as regular exercise, a balanced diet, and adequate sleep. It's also essential to avoid harmful habits such as smoking, excessive drinking, and drug use. Taking care of your physical health not only improves your overall well-being but also provides the energy and stamina you need to pursue other areas of life.

Emotional and Mental Health

Emotional and mental health are just as important as physical health, and they require balance and attention as well. Neglecting your emotional and mental health can lead to anxiety, depression, and other mental health issues that can significantly impact your happiness.

To achieve balance in this area, it is essential to prioritize self-care and stress management. This may involve seeking therapy or counseling, practicing mindfulness and meditation, or developing healthy coping mechanisms for dealing with stress and difficult emotions. It's also important to prioritize relationships and social connections, as these can provide a source of support and comfort during difficult times.

34: FINDING BALANCE: CREATING A SUSTAINABLE LIFESTYLE FOR LONG-TERM HAPPINESS

Personal Growth and Development

Personal growth and development are critical components of long-term happiness, as they allow us to pursue our passions, develop new skills, and find meaning and purpose in life. However, it's important to find balance in this area, as too much focus on personal growth can lead to burnout and overwhelm.

To achieve balance in this area, it's essential to set realistic goals and priorities, and to break down larger goals into smaller, achievable steps. It's also important to prioritize self-reflection and introspection, as this can help you gain clarity on your values, interests, and priorities. Seeking out learning opportunities, whether through formal education or informal experiences, can also help you grow and develop in meaningful ways.

Financial Stability

Financial stability is another critical component of overall happiness, as financial stress and instability can significantly impact your well-being. However, finding balance in this area requires more than just accumulating wealth or financial resources.

To achieve balance in this area, it's important to develop healthy financial habits such as budgeting, saving, and living within your means. It's also essential to prioritize financial goals that align with your values and priorities, rather than simply accumulating wealth for its own sake. Developing a healthy relationship with money and avoiding excessive materialism can also contribute to long-term financial stability and happiness.

Social Connections

Social connections are another critical component of overall happiness, as humans are social beings who thrive on connection and community. However, finding balance in this area requires more than simply surrounding yourself with people.

To achieve balance in this area, it's important to cultivate meaningful relationships that provide a sense of connection, support, and belonging. This may involve seeking out like-minded individuals or joining groups or organizations that align with your values and interests. It's also important to prioritize quality over quantity when it comes to social connections, as a few close, meaningful relationships can be more beneficial than many superficial ones.

Spiritual Well-Being

Spiritual well-being refers to a sense of connection to something greater than oneself, and it can provide a source of comfort, meaning, and purpose in life. Finding balance in this area requires more than just following a particular religious tradition, however.

To achieve balance in this area, it's important to cultivate a sense of mindfulness and presence, as well as a sense of gratitude and awe for the world around you. This may involve practices such as meditation, prayer, or nature walks, or simply taking time to appreciate the beauty and wonder of life. It's also important to align your spiritual beliefs and practices with your values and priorities, rather than simply following external traditions or expectations.

In conclusion, finding balance in life is essential for long-term happiness and well-being. Balancing work and personal life, physical and emotional health, personal growth and development, financial stability, social connections, and spiritual well-being requires intentional effort and prioritization. By developing healthy habits and practices in each of these areas, you can create a sustainable lifestyle that supports your overall happiness and fulfillment.

35: Overcoming Challenges: How to Stay Happy During Tough Times

Life is full of challenges, and they come in different shapes and sizes. They can be physical, emotional, financial, or even spiritual. And when they come knocking at our door, they can be very overwhelming and difficult to deal with. But the truth is, challenges are part of life, and how we deal with them determines our happiness and overall success in life. In this chapter, we'll explore proven strategies and practical tips for overcoming challenges and staying happy during tough times.

The first step to overcoming challenges is to accept that they exist. Denying or avoiding them will only make things worse. It's important to face your challenges head-on and deal with them effectively. This can be a difficult process, but it's the only way to move forward and grow. When we face our challenges, we gain strength and wisdom that can help us in the future.

One of the most important things to remember when facing challenges is to stay positive. It's easy to get bogged down by negative thoughts and emotions when things are tough, but a positive mindset can help us overcome even the most difficult obstacles. When we focus on the good things in our life, we can find the strength and motivation to keep going.

Another important strategy for overcoming challenges is to set realistic goals. When we're facing a big challenge, it's easy to become overwhelmed and feel like we're never going to succeed. But setting small, achievable goals can help us make progress and stay motivated. Celebrate each small victory along the way, and use them as fuel to keep moving forward.

It's also important to remember that we don't have to face our challenges alone. Seeking help from friends, family, or a professional can provide us with the support and guidance we need to overcome even the toughest obstacles. Sometimes, just talking about our problems can help us see things in a new light and come up with solutions we hadn't considered before.

When facing challenges, it's also important to take care of ourselves. This means getting enough sleep, eating a healthy diet, and exercising regularly. Taking care of our physical

health can help us feel more energized and better equipped
to deal with whatever comes our way.

In addition to taking care of our physical health, it's also important to take care of our mental and emotional well-being. This means practicing self-care activities like meditation, yoga, or journaling. Taking the time to reflect on our
thoughts and emotions can help us gain clarity and perspective, and can also help us find peace and happiness
even during tough times.

Another important strategy for overcoming challenges is to
focus on what we can control. There are some things in life
that are beyond our control, and it's easy to get caught up in
worrying about them. But when we focus on what we can
control, we can make progress and take action to improve
our situation. This can help us feel more empowered and in
control, even when things are tough.

Finally, it's important to remember that challenges can be
opportunities for growth and learning. When we face difficult situations, we have the chance to learn valuable lessons
and develop new skills. By embracing our challenges and
using them as opportunities for growth, we can become

stronger and more resilient, and we can achieve even greater happiness and success in life.

In conclusion, overcoming challenges is an essential part of living a happy and fulfilling life. By accepting that challenges exist, staying positive, setting realistic goals, seeking help, taking care of ourselves, focusing on what we can control, and embracing challenges as opportunities for growth, we can overcome even the toughest obstacles and achieve our dreams. So the next time you're faced with a challenge, remember these strategies and stay committed to your happiness and success.

36: Conclusion: Living Your Best Life Yet!

As we come to the end of this comprehensive guide to achieving true happiness, we hope that you have gained valuable insights and tools for living a fulfilling life. We have covered a lot of ground, from understanding the science of happiness to exploring practical strategies for improving your mental and emotional wellbeing.

But before we conclude, let us take a moment to reflect on the journey we have taken together. At the beginning of this book, we discussed the importance of defining what true happiness means to you. This is a crucial step in the process of achieving lasting happiness, as it enables you to align your actions with your values and aspirations.

We then explored the science of happiness, which revealed that happiness is not a fleeting emotion, but rather a state of being that can be cultivated through intentional actions and habits. We learned that happiness is not dependent on external circumstances, but rather on our internal state of mind.

With this understanding, we delved into practical strategies for improving our mental and emotional wellbeing. We learned the importance of cultivating positive emotions such as gratitude, compassion, and forgiveness, and how these emotions can enhance our overall sense of happiness and wellbeing.

We also discussed the role of mindfulness and meditation in promoting inner peace and reducing stress and anxiety. We explored practical tips for incorporating mindfulness into our daily lives, such as breathing exercises, mindful eating, and mindful listening.

Another key aspect of achieving true happiness is cultivating meaningful relationships with others. We discussed the importance of social connections and how they can enhance our overall sense of wellbeing. We explored practical tips for building and nurturing relationships, such as active listening, expressing gratitude, and setting healthy boundaries.

Finally, we discussed the importance of taking care of our physical health, including proper nutrition, exercise, and sleep. We explored practical tips for incorporating healthy habits into our daily routines, such as meal planning, setting fitness goals, and creating a relaxing bedtime routine.

36: CONCLUSION: LIVING YOUR BEST LIFE YET!

Now, armed with these insights and tools, it is up to you to take action and begin living your best life yet! Remember that happiness is a journey, not a destination. It is a lifelong process of self-discovery and growth, and it requires intentional effort and commitment.

Here are some final tips to help you along the way:

– Cultivate a growth mindset: Embrace challenges as opportunities for growth and learning, and view setbacks as temporary obstacles that can be overcome.

– Practice self-compassion: Be kind and compassionate to yourself, and treat yourself with the same care and kindness that you would offer to a friend.

– Set goals and take action: Identify your values and aspirations, and set realistic goals that align with these values. Take action towards these goals every day, even if they are small steps.

– Prioritize self-care: Take care of your physical, emotional, and mental health, and prioritize activities that bring you joy and fulfillment.

36: CONCLUSION: LIVING YOUR BEST LIFE YET!

– Build meaningful relationships: Invest in your social connections and cultivate relationships that bring you joy and support.

– Practice gratitude: Focus on the good in your life and express gratitude for the blessings that you have.

– Embrace the present moment: Let go of the past and future, and focus on the present moment. Mindfulness can help you cultivate this mindset.

In conclusion, we hope that this guide has provided you with the tools and insights you need to achieve true happiness and live your best life yet. Remember that happiness is a journey, and it requires intentional effort and commitment. But with the right mindset and tools, you can unlock the transformative power of true happiness and experience a life filled with purpose, joy, and fulfillment. Good luck on your journey!

Thank You

As we reach the end of this book, I want to say thanks for reading this book.

I want to get this information out to as many people as possible. If you found this book helpful, I would greatly appreciate you leaving me a review. This helps others find the book as well.

Disclaimer

This document is geared towards providing exact and reliable information in regards to the topic and issue covered. The publication is sold on the idea that the publisher is not required to render an accounting, officially permitted, or otherwise, qualified services. If advice is necessary, legal, financial, medical or professional, a practiced individual in the profession should be ordered.

This information is not presented by a financial or medical practitioner and is for entertainment, educational and informational purposes only. The content is not intended as a substitute for professional medical advice, diagnosis, or treatment. Always seek the advice of your physician or other qualified health care provider with any questions you may have regarding a medical condition. Never disregard professional medical advice or delay in seeking it because of something you have read.

The information provided herein is stated to be truthful and consistent, in that any liability, in terms of inattention or otherwise, by any usage or abuse of any policies, processes, or directions contained within is the solitary and utter responsibility of the recipient reader. Under no circumstances

DISCLAIMER

will any legal responsibility or blame be held against the publisher for any reparation, damages, or monetary loss due to the information herein, either directly or indirectly.